*"No happiness without order,
no order without authority,
no authority without unity."*
−A Vril Proverb

Machiavelli's *The Prince*
Available from bookstores

Please ask your local bookstore and library to carry this title
ISBN 978-0-996767705

eBook available from AdagioPress.com and WilliamDeanAGarner.com

The Prince isn't just for princes who thirst for, or are forcibly thrown into, advancement. It is a raw and bloody field manual for upper- and mid-level managers on predatorial ethics and power: what it is, how to obtain it, and what to do with it once you have found, stumbled across, or been granted it.

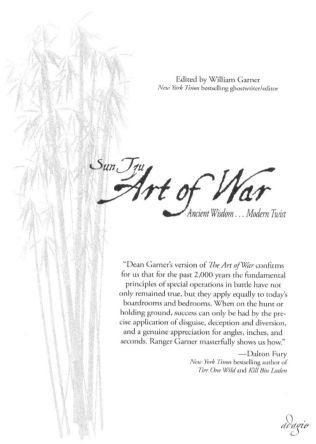

Edited by William Garner
New York Times bestselling ghostwriter/editor

Sun Tzu
Art of War
Ancient Wisdom . . . Modern Twist

"Dean Garner's version of *The Art of War* confirms
for us that for the past 2,000 years the fundamental
principles of special operations in battle have not
only remained true, but they apply equally to today's
boardrooms and bedrooms. When on the hunt or
holding ground, success can only be had by the pre-
cise application of disguise, deception and diversion,
and a genuine appreciation for angles, inches, and
seconds. Ranger Garner masterfully shows us how."

—Dalton Fury
New York Times bestselling author of
Tier One Wild and *Kill Bin Laden*

adagio

Sun Tzu *The Art of War*
Available from bookstores

Please ask your local bookstore and library to carry this title
ISBN 978-0-985536275

eBook available from AdagioPress.com and WilliamDeanAGarner.com

This contemporary edition of Sun Tzu's timeless masterpiece has
been edited down to its bare essence. It is just as, if not more,
relevant today as it was 2,500 years ago. The wisdom of *The Art of
War* teaches us that war is unnecessary. Peace is always the goal.

Burke McCarty

The Suppressed Truth About The Assassination

of Abraham Lincoln

The Suppressed Truth
About the Assassination of Abraham Lincoln
Available from bookstores

Please ask your local bookstore and library to carry this title
ISBN 978-0-996767712

eBook available from AdagioPress.com and WilliamDeanAGarner.com

Burke McCarty was a courageous ex-Catholic who conducted diligent research on the details surrounding the murder of President Abraham Lincoln by the Jesuits.

How To
1. ~~Sex it like a porn star~~
2. Write your first book
3. ~~Earn a million bucks~~
A Simple & Practical Method For
Anyone Who Can Tell A Story

New York Times bestselling ghostwriter & editor

WILLIAM GARNER

adagio

How To Write Your First Book

A Simple & Practical Method For Anyone Who Can Tell A Story

Available from bookstores

Please ask your local bookstore and library to carry this title
ISBN 978-0-985536251

eBook available from AdagioPress.com and WilliamDeanAGarner.com

Learn how to use your subconscious to dream up, develop, write and edit your first book. Garner also discusses details of the human subconscious, dreams and dreaming, and how to tap into each.

A sequel to *Who Really Owns Your Gold*, Third Edition
by New York Times bestselling ghostwriter/editor William Garner

ROMANIC DEPRESSION

How the Jesuits Designed, Built and Destroyed America

Book One

Sean Maclaren

AN INDEPENDENT PUBLISHING CRUISE

est. January 1, 2001

Katharine L. Petersen

Publisher / Senior Editor

William Dean A. Garner

Editor

Published in America by Adagio Press

Adagio and colophon are Trademarks of Adagio Press

Library of Congress Control Number: 2015957550

ISBN: 978-0-9967677-3-6

Cover design and interior: Dean Garner
Adagio website: AdagioPress.com
Email: 69@adagiopress.com

B20161126
First Print Edition

for all the beautiful souls lost in The Matrix

and for You, dear Reader

Contents

Introduction

"The Jesuits are gruesome creatures who seek
to make everyone in their own image:
physically ugly, odious and demonic. Their aim is to create a
world race of barbaric and subservient animals."
—William Garner

Romanic Depression: Book One is the first of four volumes, a multiple sequel to two previously published books: *Who Really Owns Your Gold* by William Garner and *Arcanum* by me, Sean Maclaren. Garner's *Gold* introduced how the Jesuits and their followers control and manipulate geopolitics and geoeconomics using the false notion that gold is a special and valuable tool of economic stability.

Arcanum critically reviewed a universally important set of ancient documents transcribed by disciples of Jmmanuel Sananda, the half-extraterrestrial/half-man known to the world as Jesus Christ. I detail how modern religions have distorted the truth to control and manipulate entire populations.

More than 2,000 years have passed since Jmmanuel Sananda began his teachings to a small group of disciples and followers. In many of those sermons, he foretold of a time when his words would be twisted and recast into unrecognizable forms, used to jump-start new religions and cults, and wielded as a powerful and mysterious mechanism to control large populations for malevolent purposes.

Sadly, what Jmmanuel spoke so passionately then has since become our reality.

Many of you will never see or feel this, but we are now living in the most dangerous period in the past 2,000 years. Worse than the plagues, floods, and various other biological and geological cataclysms that decimated populations of humans the world over. Those of you who live in a secure cocoon, seemingly free of the world's ills, are truly blessed.

You will never see death at the hands of an invisible assassin (influenza, HIV, Ebola, Zika), feel the misery and shame of abject poverty and despair, smell the stench of rotting bodies of children deemed "undesirables," taste the manufactured poison of fluoridated water and genetically modified corn and other deleterious products.

Mercifully, you will never sense the ongoing assault by a clever group of men who have ruled our planet from a very special place: Rome, Italy.

All Roads Lead To Rome

"All roads lead to Rome" is not some clever device to impress the uninitiated, nor is it a lamentation of those afflicted by the myriad diseases designed and built by soulless men. It is absolute fact, and this book seeks to explain how it has come to be, using dozens of concrete examples from American society today.

Even if you took just one sector and explained its design and function, and how the Jesuits control and manipulate it to their desires, most people would not believe you, much less do something to counter it. Sadly, the evolution of important occurrences here in America happens largely by the hidden hand of the Jesuits, who steer

America's sectors exactly where they want them to go.

Of the Jesuit infiltration in America in the 1800s, Author J. Wayne Laurens, in his book *The Crisis: Or the Enemies of America Unmasked*, wrote.

"And do Americans need to be told what Jesuits are? If any are ignorant, let them inform themselves of their history without delay; no time is to be lost; their workings are before you in every day's events; they are a secret society, a sort of Masonic order, with superadded features of revolting odiousness, and a thousand times more dangerous.

"They are not merely priests, or priests of one religious creed; they are merchants, and lawyers, and editors, and men of any profession, having no outward badge, (in this country) by which to be recognized; they are about in all your society.

"They can assume any character, that of angels of light, or ministers of darkness, to accomplish their one great end, the service upon which they are sent, whatever that service may be.

"They are all educated men, prepared, and sworn to start at any moment, and in any direction, and for any service, commanded by the general of their order, bound to no family, community, or country, by the ordinary ties which bind men; and sold for life to the cause of the Roman Pontiff."

How To Subjugate A Population

Please consider the following about how the current powers subjugate a country and her people, and perhaps then you will be piqued enough to consider my words further. Even if you do not believe the facts as I present them, please note this sobering fact: these actions have occurred thousands of times over hundreds of years in many different countries, they are going on as we speak, and they will continue well into the future . . . until brave souls either stop them or design and build a new system that usurps the current system.

The Jesuits and their extraterrestrial handlers are adept at infiltrating, breaking and controlling a population via these simple actions:

1. **Demoralizing** a public with depressing news in the mainstream

media, plunging the nation into serious debt to the Jesuit-controlled Federal Reserve Bank using controlled and manipulated recessions and depressions that cause high unemployment leading many to further depression and fear that often turns to anger and resentment toward the financial elite and the corporations that laid them off.

Many people in America are compelled to work more than one job to pay basic bills and living expenses, which means less or no time to spend with family and friends and less money for important things like investing for the future. Americans are pushed further into debt by abusing credit cards and taking out usurious loans they can never repay. Most people are just one paycheck away from disaster. Having less money leads to buying cheap, low-quality foods that in turn cause serious short- and long-term healthcare issues.

This lack of hope that things will improve drives many Americans to alcohol and drug abuse to cope with their sorrows, producing broken homes and divorces and our children being forced into prostitution and sex trafficking. The proliferation of drugs in our communities leads to higher crime rates and loss of personal security, among other problems.

Fear takes over and blankets the landscape.

The slow and methodical disintegration of our society and demoralizing of the public's values in the Jesuit Matrix has occurred over many years, aided by Hollywood through tv shows and movies through many different new media avenues that reach nearly everyone. This results in the erosion of moral boundaries, traditional American values and common decency.

They justify to our youth that it's okay to have loose morals, talk back to your parents and elders, act out violently like they see actors do in movies and use curse words frequently as they see people of all ages now do on tv shows.

Life imitating art.

The proliferation of today's high-drama reality shows promote the manipulation of others to win a prize. There exists today a common thread of sexually explicit themes in most tv shows, movies and even commercials, more so than any other time in our recorded history. Many tv shows and movies today also promote violence, drug abuse, murder, and intolerance and even hatred for other cultures and races to further divide the human race.

We are so desensitized and habituated to the violence we see every day in movies and on tv that we don't realize the countless ways it affects and changes us. We are being hit from every possible angle yet we are mentally numb to what is really going on around us, seemingly powerless to do anything about it. We simply accept society as how things are today without ever questioning how or why things got to be this way. And coincidentally, all of these things being used to demoralize Americans were designed to promote the growth of many Jesuit businesses and their continuing agenda here in America.

2. **Destabilizing** a population by pitting groups against each other, i.e. Democrats vs. Republicans or pro-choice vs. anti-abortion or gun owners vs. anti-gun citizens, in pitched battle. We live in the Jesuits' world of duality. And when they can't corral those elusive holdouts who subscribe to no party or religion or group, the Jesuits create even further "false and controlled opposition," i.e. those people and groups who purport to be friends and representatives of good people (I sometimes refer to us as We The People) and who allegedly oppose the Jesuits, echoing their pro-We The People sentiments in high public places, but secretly do the bidding of them.

The grim reality is that those final holdouts among We The People are cleverly being pulled into a black hole of false security by all the false and controlled opposition. Examples: Dr. Noam Chomsky, Alex Jones, Jesse Ventura, Glenn Beck, the Tea Party.

False and controlled opposition all have a national audience, slick shows and presentations with great production value and, of course, virtually unlimited funding. They reach a much larger audience than members of the true opposition movement who have a very small number of followers and whose broadcasts are intentionally throttled or disallowed altogether.

William Garner conducted an in-person interview with Dr. Noam

Chomsky in his office at MIT, in 2009. Chomsky was visibly upset over the passing of his wife, and spoke in very low tones, sometimes barely audible. What was quite clear during the hour-long discussion, however, was that Chomsky toed the party line of the Jesuits: "transnational corporations" were leading the world and controlling it economically. He dismissed Garner's assertion that the Jesuits were the human controllers of the planet, and offered little else.

3. **Orchestrating crisis after crisis**, e.g. false-flag attacks on America's shores, mass shootings, internecine wars, regional wars, global wars. Throughout history we've been manipulated by the Jesuits using the so-called Problem-Reaction-Solution paradigm in creating false-flag events. It is best described as a strategy that creates a crisis to justify an action.

The three basic parts of this paradigm are:

1. The Jesuits create a crisis, such as a terror attack or economic collapse (Problem).

2. The American people then react to the crisis, asking or even demanding the government for help, which usually involves giving up their rights and liberties in the process (Reaction).

3. With the population properly conditioned, the government then offers a "solution" to the crisis. Of course, the solution was planned long before the crisis ever happened (Solution).

The Problem-Reaction-Solution scenario is a label concocted by the Jesuits and pandered about by their "controlled opposition" media soldiers.

The scenario is more accurately termed what I call Attack-Response-Subjugation, as it depicts the whole Jesuit scenario in a stark light. It is the tool of choice when they want to introduce a law or conflict that they know will be greatly opposed by the population. The purpose is not to solve Americans' problems, but to serve the Jesuit agenda; it is a means to an end.

There are thousands of examples of this in human history, repeated over and over to great success, yet the American people remain oblivious to them.

Some notable examples of glaring false-flag attacks, not limited to America:

The explosion of the *USS Maine* (1898), sinking of the *RMS Lusitania* (1915), Reichstag fire in Germany (1933), assassination of President John F. Kennedy (1963), Gulf of Tonkin incident (1964), attack on the *USS Liberty* (1967), World Trade Center bombings (1993), Oklahoma City bombings (1995), 9/11 bombings (2001), and Sandy Hook shooting (2012).

The Jesuits also planned and instigated World War I (1914-1918), The Great Depression (1929-1939), World War II (1939-1945), Persian Gulf War (1990-1991), Iraq War (2003-2011), "War on Terror," illegal attacks on nations like Afghanistan and Iraq, culminating in forced military occupation of those nations.

False-flag attacks on American soil, targeting innocent civilians, are now the norm today, with mass shootings of civilians and law-enforcement officers occurring at least several times a month. Overseas, the shootings in Paris, France serve as a prime example of a Jesuit false-flag attack resulting in several different western nations attacking Muslims throughout the world, in particular the Middle East where war rages on in Syria. Some call this the beginning of World War III.

4. **Forcing legislation** that removes basic Constitutional rights. An excellent and unfortunate example: United Nations Framework Convention on Climate Change effectively destroys the entire US Constitution. The Patriot Act is rife with hidden entries that have nothing to do with national security and further remove our rights as citizens. These two acts alone render Americans without any rights at all.

The passage of illegal and frightening legislation like the National Defense Authorization Act of 2013 (NDAA), part of which reads, "the indefinite detention of American citizens by the military without due process at the discretion of the President" whether you are in the USA or traveling to another country.

Already in progress: the confiscation of guns, weapons and ammunition, shortage of black powder for ammunition. This process has been slow and methodical, but definite and involved the National Rifle Association, a false and controlled group set up by the Jesuits.

Please keep in mind that the Jesuits operate over years and decades, slowly and methodically advancing their positions.

Recall the words of Lord Robert Montagu: "The little step, long continued—the very gradual but persistent advance—is sure to attain its end."

5. **Normalizing** a population, allowing those in power to bring the American public under its sphere of influence, bringing to a screeching halt all protests against the regime, eliminating all challengers, and thus fully subjugating the people.

Since 9/11, the Jesuits have greatly accelerated their program, which normally runs over 50-100 years and goes unnoticed by the population.

Using this simple yet highly effective method of Attack-Response-Subjugation, the Jesuits have turned America into a gaudy billboard in paradise. Consider these observations from afar: foreigners who keep well informed about world events see America as a spoiled bratty child, ill-informed, ignorant of world matters, uncaring of others outside the sandbox.

America commands no respect outside her borders, because she sees other countries as mere distant, bastard suburbs of New York City. It is not good people like you who are to blame. Far from it. However, we have been trained to act the bratty and spoiled child, so others outside our borders despise us so and create a great rift between good Americans and their peers all over the world.

It's not our fault. Americans are programmed this way by BigMedia, BigAdvertising, BigEntertainment, BigPharma, BigLaw, BigMoney, BigFood and BigEducation, etc.

A Brief History Of How This Book Series Was Conceived

When embarking on any journey, I first do extensive research about the areas where I'll be traveling, the people and animals I'll likely encounter, inherent dangers and hazards, various languages spoken and customs used, and then do "active dream journeys" in a relaxed state, where I image (no, not imagine) myself in all situations I am likely to experience.

The result is a series of likely outcomes, which I store away for further study and use. In this way, I can see the end fairly clearly. But even more important, I can see the many paths I can possibly take along the way.

When considering a new venture, most people see the end in mind, and we're taught that this is the best way to succeed. I say this is incorrect. We also must see the many different paved roads, unimproved paths, and territories untouched. That is, we must consider the unknown means, as well.

More than 40 years ago, my mentor William Garner found himself in a Catholic military school in San Antonio, Texas (Mount Sacred Heart Military Academy), one his mother insisted he attend while his father was flying night missions in the F-4D over Vietnam.

During his time there, enduring the punishments of the "sisters of God," he often wondered why Catholicism, a religion so "special," as the nuns put it, had to be pounded into his little body so violently and painfully.

And why did that priest have to force himself on that beautiful little nun as he did, raping her into submission? Was it all in the name of God?

According to written testimony over 2,000 years, various Roman clergy have used their religion to beat populations to a pulp, and to abuse their power to rape men, women and children, and sometimes dispose of their bodies in secret mass graves.

According to the Catholics, yes, it was all in the name of the being they worshipped, the man they called Jesus Christ and the spirit they worshipped: God.

Jmmanuel Sananda warned us about this typical behavior by those who would use his words to control and oppress people all over the world.

William Garner saw it first hand in 3rd grade, in that Catholic military school for boys, where they were punished daily for simple "wrongs," and nuns were raped by priests for . . . reasons perhaps never to be discovered, although the practice of forced sexual acts upon the population is well documented by independent researchers and authors in many different countries over centuries. Such glaring corroboration needs no further introduction.

Needless to say, William Garner dropped any interest in this so-called religion at the age of seven. It was a conscious (and subconscious) choice he made, because he wanted to explore something outside this current life that so constrained him.

Mr. Garner explained to me: "I would look up at the deep-blue night sky, see the stars bursting and playing in front of me, and imagine myself on a journey into the black beyond. I could only get so far until I realized I wasn't equipped to handle what I may encounter. So I stopped all Universal ventures and decided I would limit my travels to Mother Earth, which provided more than enough engrossing passages and chapters to fill many books.

"My personal journey was not to uncover the details underlying what I encountered and experienced. I wanted nothing more of those indignities. This mission of mine transcended all paths already taken, and placed me on an entirely new azimuth, one I never could have predicted on any level.

"Just over 30 years ago, I was accosted by a man whose spark ignited a small brush fire that would set me on this new journey of discovery. It was at an embassy party in Washington, DC: lovely young women and men serving the treats of their country's famous cuisine, men of intense martial character attempting to steal secrets from various military attaches, and one lone man dashing across the room to accost me and exclaim, 'He'll be the death of us all!'

"Never mind that I had just been attacked by an unknown assailant, I was more excited to find out what the blazes he was talking about, so I asked, 'Who?'

" 'Brzezinski!' [Zbigniew Brzezinski]

"Over the next few decades, I did anecdotal research in libraries and personal collections, going from one rabbit hole to the next, gathering information and intelligence on what I would later see as an extensive network of very clever people who ran the daily operations of our entire planet.

"From Brzezinski to the House of Rothschild and beyond, I followed the trail of something far more than mere gold and money. This was a grand conspiracy, the likes of which had never been seen or spoken of. And yet it was being seen everywhere and by everyday lay people. They just didn't know it or out of fear did not speak or write about it. And yet elements of it were being shared in all countries. The citizens just couldn't quite comprehend and articulate it, let alone put a face to it, but they knew something was amiss.

"When I observed and studied the behavioral ecology of the Jesuits, I felt like I was witnessing a physically ugly 12-year-old boy caught in a lie. He defended his lie to the bitter end, even though circumstances proved him dead wrong.

"I was observing the behavior of a vicious little animal. In human moral terms, a psychopath. It bothered me to no end but, then again, I enjoy studying things that bother me, little things that sting and bite and cause annoying itches that keep me up at night. They're all trying to tell me something important, and I have an obligation to investigate.

"I've found that Americans tend to avoid subjects (especially in books) they can't comprehend. They are willing to listen to or read about large international corporations, the Rothschilds and the Morgans, Bill Gates and Warren Buffett, but certainly not the Jesuits. The Society of Jesus rules the world!? That is absurd to the vast majority of Americans, many of whom openly attack me and my findings, while unknowingly support the Jesuits, those hidden creatures who enslave them. Worst of all, it is Americans' glittering inaction to extricate themselves from this voluntary slavery that proves my point."

All of William Garner's work brings me to this new volume of work, the culmination of eyewitness experiences, in-depth research, meetings with those in the know, communications with insiders and whistleblowers, analyzing all those BigData, and compiling them into one coherent volume of knowledge for all to consider.

The Pitfalls Of Taking On The Jesuits

Romanic Depression isn't merely one of two sequels to a previous work, *Who Really Owns Your Gold*, it is new episode into this subject, a roll call of epic Jesuit crimes in America that continue to the day and, in fact, are worsening with time.

I have chosen to break up this book into a series of shorter books for easy reading. Seems most people these days prefer sound bites to full-length books, mostly because they just don't have the time to read, let alone study this subject at length.

Fascinating as it is, studying grand conspiracies is the most depressing subject and field of study I could possibly encounter, yet it draws me in so. It takes a thick skin and an air of pure objectivity. Even armed with the two, one must endure the vicissitudes and vagaries of the world of conspiracies day in and day out. Many places I look, I know there is something sinister going on behind the scenes, and it is cleverly manipulated by the Jesuits.

Again, it can be downright depressing, especially dealing with Jesuits and their followers, but I find it all most fascinating and intriguing.

Someone once told me that 1% of the people will love you (if you are fortunate), 1% of the people will hate you, and 98% just won't care.

I say to that person now that you were flat wrong: 99.999% of those I attempt to reach with my accurate facts will dismiss me outright. This statistic alone should bring great comfort to the Jesuits, their handlers and all the followers who serve them.

In times of any crisis, there must be brave and courageous people who take on the enemy full force. Each generation should have representatives who carry on the fight.

There are so few of these brave souls today, because the Jesuits and their extraterrestrial handlers have so cleverly drugged the good people of this world with poisoned pharmaceuticals, food, water and air that virtually no one is of sound mind and body, much less a formidable warrior who could possibly confront and defeat them.

Where is the next generation of young souls who will take on these powerful entities?

They're glued to PlayStation or Xbox or the next big gaming tool, apending whole nights and weekends watching Netflix movie marathons, Hulu, endless YouTube videos or listening to iTunes, they are one with their iPad or smart phones, and they get all their news and information from the very entity that enslaves them.

> "The Matrix is a system, Neo. That system is our enemy, and when you're inside and look around, what do you see? Businessmen, teachers, lawyers, carpenters, the very minds of the people we are trying to save. But until we do, these people are still a part of that system and that makes them our enemy. You have to understand: most of these people are not ready to be unplugged, and many of them are so inured, so hopelessly dependent on the system, that they will fight to protect it."
> —Morpheus, in The Matrix

Allow me to repeat that: they get all of their news and information from the very entity that enslaves them. It's a vicious cycle that keeps them unaware of the accurate truth and convinces them to vigorously defend the lies of the Jesuits.

This is all by clever design.

When someone like me comes along to disrupt their knowledge and experience, they immediately attack the messenger, the very person who is trying to wake them up from this deep, drug-induced sleep. Without realizing it, they go on the offensive in droves and swarms to destroy a sober voice of reason and sanity.

It is time for others to join me and take up this fight and uncover and disseminate the thousands of facts, books, artifacts, and absolute proof about the ancient knowledge that has been suppressed for more than 2,000 years by a group of very weak people who use clever tools and processes to control a much more powerful and numerous group of human beings.

There exist many instances of suppressed knowledge all over the world, some of it on the Internet in various forms. It is time for others to seek this out, make good sense of it, implement what they can, teach others to use it wisely, and ensure that the current powers cannot further enslave the rest of us. I surely cannot do this alone.

It is said everyday that one person can do one small thing, perform one seemingly insignificant act that can change the world.

I have seen these miracles over the years, most of which have been caught and suppressed by the powers before these gifts could take proper hold in the population and reach critical mass, a tipping point beyond which we see a great shift in some area that positively affects millions of people.

The current powers are quick and effective at suppressing even the smallest of potential threats to their schemes, so we must design effective ways to counter them. The best method appears to be by volume, i.e. using millions of beautiful souls to effect a desired outcome.

The Jesuits have used this technique many times, provoking millions of people to react to a certain event, which produces a very real physical energy that can be stored and used for other purposes. Recent examples include the murders of very good people: entertainers Anton Yelchin, Prince, Paul Walker, Joan Rivers, Whitney Houston and Robin Williams. All were—are still—greatly admired and loved by millions of people. When the news of each person's death was announced, their was a great outpouring of shock, sorrow, anger and rage all at once that produced a very real physical energy in different parts of the world, one that could have been measured if one had chosen to do so.

How To Study The Jesuits

There are forces beyond our human comprehension, very real physical forces that are tightly controlled by the Jesuits, who have created a dumbed-down version of the actual Universal reality that exists beyond our human borders. William Garner calls Earth-based physics "sandbox physics," and this is an accurate term, because it describes the elementary and even false version of the real Universal discipline that is currently beyond our reach and comprehension.

Again, it is time for brave souls to take a keen interest in the world around them, ask hard questions like "Who runs our world and how do they do it?" and "What can I do now to learn about these powerful forces?"

Even in the absence of knowing that these brave people exist now, I am forever hopeful that they will appear in the near future and will take up the fight against a very powerful (yet truly weak) enemy.

Those people who take on this task will uncover spellbinding details not found in even the most compelling and captivating novels about magic and vampires and the supernatural. Truth isn't only stranger than fiction, it is so real that you can reach out and touch and experience it. You can drop yourself into a grand waking dream of unimaginable fantasy, rocket off to another world where up is down, black is white, and nothing is what it first appears.

A clue for you: the current powers are bound by strict Universal laws to reveal to us humans the coming or presence of some of their actions. Trick is, we just have to discover them. They're out there, some obvious, most not so. We see them mostly in news and advertising by BigMedia, tv shows and movies by BigEntertainment. But they're also there in plain sight, in everyday visuals and sounds, scents and tastes.

How do you discover something about which you know nothing?

Another clue: you have all the answers inside you. You just need to ask the right questions and summon your subconscious to assist you in discovering the answers.

This is not a riddle, nor is it some cruel joke.

Jmmanuel Sananda spoke of this Universal rule. Since we are one with Creation and The Universe, we have all the knowledge of both. The great misfortune is that the Jesuits and their extraterrestrial handlers have taught us to believe that we are ignorant fools who are incapable of knowing anything beyond what they feed us via BigMedia and BigEntertainment.

Our very own DNA, most of which we are told is "junk," contains the "knowledge" of millions (if not billions and more!) of years and the experience of all others who have come before us. There is also Universal knowledge stored in many other parts of our brain and body, although the current powers have told us otherwise.

Doubtless you have heard how light and sound can greatly affect our behaviors, experiences and overall mental and physical health. This Universal knowledge has been suppressed by various Roman powers over the millennia, and remains largely hidden from us.

Imagine the superpowers you have deep within you, well within your reach, if you would only take the time to discover and study them, and implement what you've learned. Billions of people all over the world would suddenly wake up, look around, see a land of new possibilities and opportunities, and watch as the old Jesuit regime crumbled.

I would be remiss if I did not share with you some of the things you will experience on my guided journey. Some of you have already read about Jmmanuel Sananda and his extant sermons, his wishes and desires for, and commandments to all of mankind, including my personal assessment (a psychoanalysis) of those sermons, plus 124 Laws of Creation and The Universe I extracted from Jmmanuel's sermons.

The Big Irony: The Jesuits Are Not Traitors To America

Those in power are not traitors to the American people. They are employees of a formal corporation, based in Rome and controlled by the Jesuits and their ET masters. All employees of this corporation and its subsidiaries are beholden only to the corporation, not to American citizens.

Therefore, the employees of this corporation are not traitors to Americans any more than those who advertise products on behalf of Apple or Microsoft are to their customers.

We Americans must understand the playing field and the rules of the game, which are partly determined by corporate laws, codes, rules and regulations that apply to Americans. In certain cases, employees of the corporation are exempt from these same laws that govern the actions and behaviors of Americans.

When Americans have business with this corporation or any of its subsidiaries, those Americans can choose not to do business with this corporation. Given the corporation has established itself as a shadow government inside specified borders where Americans live, it is next to impossible not to do some form of business with the corporation.

The alternative is to move beyond the borders and live elsewhere, only to be subjected to the laws, rules and regulations of still another corporation, acting as a shadow government of that other country.

Until we Americans understand the nature of the game, we will continue to whine unnecessarily and essentially get nothing done toward ending this madness.

Learn the game, play the game, manipulate the game to your advantage. It all starts with learning and understanding.

Romanic Depression: From Soup To Nuts

What follows now is the outcome of more than 2,000 years of actions and behaviors by the very sinister forces Jmmanuel spoke of, those who bastardized his words and teachings, and created a whole new world of pain and suffering, oppression and subjugation, and long-lasting destruction and ruin.

In this new book series, *Romanic Depression*, I have taken more than 40 subjects (sectors of society) you're well familiar with, and reported on the state of the art for each area, paying particular attention to how the Jesuits and their extraterrestrial handlers have designed each area to fit their overall agenda.

Again, this is a series of several books, each with 10 or so chapters. Each chapter focuses on a particular subject or sector of American society, and could easily fill a 500-page book unto itself. However, I have chosen to present to you a reasonable digest of each subject area, with the hope it will spark your interest and prompt you to pursue further study. I also pray that the shorter nature of these books will allow for sufficient study, digestion and analysis, so you develop a keen insight into the corrupt power structure of America and our planet.

There are only two ways to prove a conspiracy: the conspirators or insiders or whistleblowers come forward with direct evidence, or someone like me does first-rate research over many years, gathering and corroborating evidence of circumstances from many different sources, analyzing those data to the nth degree and making sense of it, then compiling the results and presenting them to a worldwide audience for their consideration.

In researching all topics, I have employed the same true method as with William Garner's previous research and writings, using direct evidence from person observations, eyewitness reports from trusted researchers, insiders, whistleblowers, anonymous donors, and primary-source materials, and circumstantial evidence from many different sources.

In beginning your studies, I heartily suggest you employ William Garner's method of extreme "binge research," i.e. reading and taking in as much information as possible at once, which allows the subconscious to absorb vast amounts of intelligence in a very short period of time and distill it down to its very essence. The subconscious needs a lot of intel to process a small final end product of digested information.

When Garner used this method to analyze the works of Shakespeare, he discovered five distinct voices in those writings. According to Garner, at least five Jesuits wrote the works of Shakespeare, which were designed to manipulate all sectors of European society and establish strict Roman standards.

When studying a particular subject, I read 10 books in a week and, if possible, by the same author back to back. This method allows me to discover subtle cues and nuances that would otherwise be lost if I only read a book a week.

I also study the Jesuits in three ways: 1. Use the good work of others directly; 2. Stand on the shoulders of good researchers and develop new hypotheses; and 3. Discover entirely new facts on my own.

Use Your Brilliant Mind To Study And Comprehend

We underestimate the grand power of the human subconscious, so much so that you are probably dismissing me outright at this moment. Please take the time to dump large bundles of data into your subconscious at once, so it can do the bulk of the work for you, that is, make accurate sense of a very difficult subject.

You do not have to be a trained scientist to do good research, but you must be diligent, patient, discerning and persnickety in your work. Please trust your subconscious to guide you.

For further information about how to use your subconscious to do the work for you, please consult William Garner's book *How To Write Your First Book*. There are chapters on the human subconscious, dreams and dreaming, and how to use your inner tools to work for you. It's a fascinating process, and I strongly encourage you to discover it.

My express wish for you and those you love and care for is that you all, regardless of age, take an interest in who runs your world and how they do it. From there, start asking your own questions, and do your own research, analyze the results of your work, talk it over with family and friends and colleagues, try to make sense of it, then share it with the world and see how others react.

Encourage them to consider your thoughts and ideas, your personal findings and discoveries, and encourage further thought and action.

WARNING: most of those you reach out to will ignore you and dismiss you outright. Others, however—maybe just a handful—will have that special spark inside them, something ignited by your inspiring words, that grows into a huge brush fire that in turn stimulates and calls others to action.

My eternal hope is that I have inspired you to move forth and conquer ignorance, reveal the accurate truth, and forge a new and prosperous paradise for all. I leave you momentarily with a grand passage by Thomas Paine who, even 200 years ago, was already lamenting and contemplating the decline and eventual fall of America. Although Paine never publicly wrote about the Jesuits, his words protested against them and their despotic rule:

"When we contemplate the fall of empires, and the extinction of the nations of the ancient world, we see but little more to excite our regret than the mouldering ruins of pompous palaces, magnificent monuments, lofty pyramids, and the walls and towers of the most costly workmanship; but when the empire of America shall fall, the subject for contemplative sorrow will be infinitely greater than crumbling brass or marble can inspire.

"It will not then be said, Here stood a temple of vast antiquity, here rose a Babel of invisible height, or there a palace of sumptuous magnificence; but here . . . the noblest work of human wisdom, the greatest scene of human glory, the fair cause of freedom, rose and fell!"

What Other Brave Researchers Have Said About The Jesuits

Hundreds of other researchers have published scathing commentaries on the malevolent behavior of the Jesuits, and most of those books have been destroyed, suppressed or lost over considerable time. One of the most vociferous opponents of the Jesuits was Giovanni

Battista Nicolini, who authored the 1854 book *History of the Jesuits: Their Origin, Progress, Doctrines, and Designs.* He said:

"The Jesuits, by their very calling, by the very essence of their institution, are bound to seek, by every means, right or wrong, the destruction of Protestantism. This is the condition of their existence, the duty they must fulfill, or cease to be Jesuits."

Unfortunately, Nicolini was only partly accurate. Actually, the Jesuits were not simply after Protestants to bring them back into the fold, they were after any person, group or organization that opposed the Jesuits. Through the pope's claim of "infallibility," the Church (and hence the Jesuits that controlled and manipulated it) owned every single person and thing across the planet. In short, the pope could do no harm, was all-knowing, and the supreme ruler over all.

President Abraham Lincoln, who was murdered by the Jesuits, said this about the pope and Jesuits:

"I feel more and more every day that it is not against the Americans of the South alone I am fighting. It is more against the Pope of Rome, his perfidious Jesuits and their blind and bloodthirsty slaves, than against American Protestants . . . It is Rome who wants to rule and degrade the North, as she has ruled and degraded the South from the very day of its discovery.

"She divides our nation in order to weaken, subdue, and rule it. [Samuel F.B.] Morse has told me of the plots made in Rome to undermine our institutions and our laws, destroy our schools, and prepare a reign of anarchy here, as they have done in Ireland, in Mexico, in Spain, and wherever there are any people who want to be free."

He also shared with Reverend Charles Chiniquy in his book *Fifty Years in the Church of Rome* a prophetic thought about the Jesuits being exposed:

"I do not pretend to be a prophet. But though not a prophet I see a very dark cloud on our horizon. And that dark cloud is coming from Rome. It is filled with the tears of blood. It will rise and increase, till its flanks are torn by a flash of lightning, followed by a fearful peal of thunder.

"Then a cyclone such as the world has never seen, will pass over this country, spreading ruin and desolation from north to south. After it is over, there will be long days of peace and prosperity: for Popery, with its Jesuits and merciless Inquisition, will have been swept away from our country. Neither I nor you, but our children, will see those things."

Please read Adagio Press's new versions of *The Suppressed Truth About the Assassination of Abraham Lincoln* and Chiniquy's *Fifty Years in the Church of Rome* to learn more about how the Jesuits plotted and executed a grand plan to murder America's beloved President Lincoln and create an enduring fiction about his assassination.

Be inspired to take strong, positive action that, in turn, propels others to do even more. Remember: the ills of America and the world do not happen without clever and deliberate design, leadership, guidance and trillions of dollars each year. Only you and like-minded people can counter them.

My aim with *Romanic Depression* is to provide you a list of details on the behaviors and actions of those who control nearly every aspect of all sectors of our society today. Hopefully, you will be inspired to do your own research, discovering for yourself things you never thought possible. And when done, pass on your new-found discoveries to other good people.

I

The American Government: Doomed From Its Inception

"Long, long ago, King Henry of England told Prince Hal
that the way to run a country and keep the people from
being too critical of how you run it, is to busy giddy minds
with foreign quarrels."

—Dan Smoot, in *The Invisible Government*

One of the first steps toward establishing a civilization's government or ruling body, with its attendant departments, is securing land that, even today, is usually executed by force and mandated by false treaty under the guise of some forced "international law."

The area is secured using a strong military presence, normally UN troops in armored vehicles, backed up by a private military force (now special-operations forces) equipped to handle any incursions by foreign invaders and border raiders.

Once the force has established a secure stronghold, a form of government is established, with its accompanying rule of law that serves as an effective control over the population. Of course, all of these steps were planned well in advance, years even, and carried out swiftly and efficiently.

The Modern Government: Designed To Fail

Today, all governments are tightly controlled by one human entity and its extraterrestrial handlers. Each government was carefully designed and constructed, its leaders identified, groomed and emplaced not on merit or popular vote but by their degree of subservience (first), personal chemistry (second) and public charisma (third).

The US government is no different. From its inception, it was blueprinted and controlled by dynastic men hidden deep within the Roman system, built by highly malleable proteges, administered by well-trained minions, and maintained by highly ignorant people whose loyalty was unparalleled, if not radical (read: patriotic).

Perditorus Rex: A Blueprint For The New American Colonies

The Jesuits prepared to pave over the paradise that was America in several distinct steps over 170 or so years, a long-term project that was conceived by the Black Pope and his Jesuit militia in Rome, and carefully written down as a "playbook" in 1773, known only to a handful of Jesuits.

William Garner hypothesizes that the Black Pope Lorenzo Ricci did not languish and die in a Roman prison, in 1775, as revisionist history tells us, but rather, with the expert assistance of fellow Jesuits, faked his own death, traveled to America, and became the puppet master who acted behind the scenes for many years, using the playbook Garner calls *Perditorus Rex*.

Ricci and the Jesuits made 50- and 100-year plans, the general outlines of which are still being used to this day because they have proven so efficacious. If one studies the Jesuits' methods of subjugating a country, they will discover a striking pattern of similarities among all take-overs.

How To Build A Nation In Four Easy Steps
Step One: Kill the Indigenous Population

The Jesuits first sent over early scouts to kill off and subjugate the indigenous population, then established a "white-man's foothold" on the soil of the New World. The settlers carried with them new diseases originating from the farming regions of the Old World, which served to sicken and kill tens of millions of Native Americans.

Although not seen in any modern revisionist history books, the scouts traveled up and down the eastern seaboard in search of indigenous Indian populations to decimate, using the greatest tools of warfare: the virus.

This invisible band of warriors, the small pox and influenza viruses, among other cultivated viruses and bacteria, killed more people in a short period of time than any natural geologic disaster or seasoned army could ever have done in years of continuous war. The Jesuits knew the power of the Plague and wielded it like a nuclear device. The murdering of Native Americans was ethnic cleansing at its most efficacious.

Curiously, during the initial days of the Black Plague that sacked more than half the population of Europe, hundreds of black-robed men were seen carrying dark sacks emitting a "putrid odor." The Black Plague was systematically spread by these Roman members of the church, which, hundreds of years later, farmed out its game to America, to kill the natives and pave the way for future settlements by marauding Europeans.

Over the first several decades of European rule, the leftover denizens of the eastern seaboard were trained to fear the white man and his deadly cargo of disease and modern weaponry. Those who were not killed by the great viral bomb were either enslaved or forced to settle in habitats ruled undesirable to the white man.

Either way, the Native Americans lost their lives, homes and livelihood to the invading white warriors from Europe, a deeply disturbing fact that continues to this day.

Step Two: Establish Rule

Following the initial first wave of scouts in America, the Jesuits sent its next contingent, America's future despots and controllers, which occupied Jamestown, Virginia and soon spread to Maryland, Pennsylvania, Massachusetts, New York and beyond. The Jesuits used the old method that was highly effective in controlling the elite: conscription of "bloodlines."

In ancient England, there were no so-called "bloodlines," which were an ingenious invention of Romish powers. In forming the leadership of America, the Jesuits used consanguineous men and women as puppets, while the Jesuits controlled and manipulated activities behind the public spectacles.

These Europeans, most of whom were slaves to the Jesuits, brought with them their own slaves and indentured servants, some of whom escaped into the wild countryside and formed their own groups and small colonies that would later become villages and towns.

An unwanted side effect of this new wave of immigration of the ruling class was the inclusion of smart, thinking anarchists among the servants who specifically despised their owners and generally opposed any type of government rule. After all, their rights had been stripped so they could serve their masters, so these slaves were in no mood to be ruled by anyone, let alone a new form of government that did nothing to protect their rights as human beings and then continued to enslave them in paradise.

These early dissidents were a constant thorn in the side of the Jesuits, who continually tried to kill them off but eventually found a more effective way to deal with the opposition: infiltrate their groups and control them from within. We see this strategy especially today, and it plays out most effectively.

Step Three: Establish Religion

The Jesuits then focused on planting the seeds of Roman Catholicism in the New World, using staunch Catholics from largely Protestant England, which was in the throes of a decidedly anti-Catholic epoch under the rule of Queen Elizabeth I and her successor James I.

The first expedition set sail for America in November 1578 with seven ships and 350 men. They were forced to turn back after encountering fierce storms and members of the Spanish Armada.

A second attempt at bringing Catholicism to America began on June 11, 1583, when Sir Humphrey Gilbert led five ships and 200 men to the New World, four ships landing in Newfoundland two months later. Two months following the initial landing, Gilbert set sail for Maine, lost all supplies off his best ship, and then attempted to return to England. On the way, his ship and all hands were lost during a heavy storm. A companion ship returned to England to report the losses.

The first successful landing of a large contingent of Catholics in America was in 1605, after the *Archangel* made landfall on an island off the coast of Maine. The best they could do, though, was to plant several crosses in the ground, before returning to England.

England's former Secretary of State, George Calvert, retired from political life in England and was sent by the Jesuits to Virginia, where he attempted to mingle with established leaders who, it seems, wanted nothing to do with him. So he returned home where the Jesuits had the crown of England grant Calvert a patent on considerable land that would later become the state of Maryland.

He soon became the first Lord of the Jesuit city of Baltimore, and set the stage for the first mass arrival of those who would establish Catholicism as a tightly controlled religion in the New World. I discuss the early history of religion in America, in Chapter 3, American Religion: Chain of Sorrows.

Step Four: Flood the New World With Subservient Roman Catholics

After the Jesuits emplaced their band of government and religious leaders, the next step was to seed the New World with subservient citizens who would do their bidding at any time and for a song. For this, the Jesuits turned to their favorite minions, the rabid Catholics of Northern Ireland.

Long a tool of Rome, the Irish were also known to the Jesuits as a genetically aggressive and ravenous race, easily controlled with religion, drink and moderate threats. The Jesuits had long conquered Ireland and enslaved its population. Its own leaders were eager to please their Jesuit masters.

The first ripples of Irish immigrants fell on America's shores in the 1600s, where they made their way from Caribbean isles that housed Irish and Scottish criminals and misfits. Around 1720, a larger wave arrived and continued on for about 100 years. The majority of them arrived between 1820 and 1845 and settled in large strictly Irish ghettos in New York and Boston and in the Appalachian mountains, where the Scots-Irish became known as the original American "rednecks," rabble-rousers and home-grown terrorists. In later years, they would be used in some of America's first false-flag attacks on its own citizens. They moved southward into the Carolinas, Georgia and into the Louisiana Territory, where they established a firm foothold and quickly grew in numbers.

Arthur M. Schlesinger, Jr. wrote about how Irish were strongly tethered to Rome, in his 1998 book *The Disuniting of America, Reflections on a Multicultural Society*:

"These immigrants came principally from western and northern Europe. The Anglos often disliked the newcomers, disdained their uncouth presence, feared their alien religions and folkways. The Irish were regarded as shiftless and drunken; moreover, they were papists, and their fealty to Rome, it was said, meant they could never become loyal Americans. They were subjected to severe discrimination in employment and were despised by genteel society.

"As the flow of immigrants increased, so did resentment among the old-timers. By the 1850s immigrants made up half the population of New York and outnumbered native-born Americans in Chicago."

The Jesuits' method of population transfer forced or coerced Irish citizens onto ships bound for the New World. The Jesuits paid their way, gave them modest seed money, a place to live and plenty of back-breaking work. After all, there were cities to build.

These Irish-Americans were tightly controlled by the Jesuits, who emplaced priests among the population to organize them into specific groups: secondary religious leaders, community leaders, paramilitary soldiers and operators, businessmen and other professionals. As their numbers grew in each major city, the Irish quickly ensconced themselves in government, law enforcement and fire-fighting professions, which allowed the Jesuits to control and manipulate the populations of entire cities and towns. It is no surprise that the Irish also established the first gangs that later became part of the Jesuits' organized crime network we still see today.

Michael J.F. McCarthy wrote about how the Irish were ruled by the Jesuits, in his 1912 book *The Nonconformist Treason*:

"It was a Unionist Government who gave Lord MacDonnell the Under Secretaryship, which proves that he suffered nothing by Unionist Sectarianism. He has had no experience of the self-governing Colonies, he is a Jesuit-educated Roman Catholic, and, while he was Irish Under Secretary, he literally ruled Ireland through the Jesuits— his brother being at the same time an Irish Nationalist member! And how can coercion be a true description of the Unionist policy, when it was the Unionists who gave Ireland her Local Government and Land Purchase?"

How America Was Doomed From The Beginning

Some of the so-called Founding Fathers were a group of sycophants and cowards who took orders either directly from Rome or its public face, the British Crown. True, there were some brave men and women (behind the scenes) among them who genuinely opposed Jesuit rule, and this is why they originally came to America from despotic countries, but few of them ever spoke out publicly against the Jesuits, only venturing the occasional glancing blow that had little effect on its intended target.

Those who openly opposed the Jesuits were silenced, either by threats, assaults or outright murder of themselves and their family members. Many who wrote about Jesuit intrigues did so under pseudonyms, although one is hard pressed to find even one copy of their books in existence today, as the Jesuits were diligent about locating and destroying any book, pamphlet, newspaper or other printed material that openly opposed or criticized their rule or any of their actions. Foreign observers appeared to be the only successful dissenters, often publishing their research findings anonymously in books that were later smuggled into America to warn of the coming storm, not that anyone was listening.

Thomas Jefferson knew from the beginning that the Jesuits were in full control of America, because it was their pet project, one carefully planned decades in advance by Rome. By design, America was built to extract the natural resources of its lands, using slave labor, which would be used to forge the most formidable power on the planet, a slow and methodical process that would take more than 200 years.

When one considers the sheer length of time alone, it feels daunting. However, you must understand that the Jesuits and all other Roman predecessors operated on 50- and 100-year plans, even longer. The continuity of their operations was ensured by strict rules and regulations that were passed on from one generation to the next, one man to his sons and cousins, and so on.

Considering long-term projects then, it is quite easy to envision how the Jesuits masterminded the designing and building of a completely new country, including importing the seeds of its citizenry from old stock, and controlling and manipulating, if not destroying outright, the Native Americans who simply got in the way.

Even shortly after the Revolutionary War in America, Jefferson spoke shamefully of the inevitable decline of his beloved new world, America:

"The spirit of the times may alter, will alter. Our rulers will become corrupt, our people careless. A single zealot may become persecutor, and better men be his victims. It can never be too often repeated that the time for fixing every essential right, on a legal basis, is while our rulers are honest, ourselves united.

"From the conclusion of this war we shall be going down hill. It will not then be necessary to resort every moment to the people for support. They will be forgotten, therefore, and their rights disregarded. They will forget themselves in the sole faculty of making money, and will never think of uniting to effect a due respect for their rights.

"The shackles, therefore, which shall not be knocked off at the conclusion of this war, will be heavier and heavier, till our rights shall revive or expire in a convulsion."

The American War Of Independence: A Colossal Sham

We are taught that America fought and eventually won wars of independence from England, but the reality is that our "victory" was a carefully staged series of events that created only the illusion of freedom and liberty among the American people, and actually delivered something altogether different: a subjugated system well on its way to becoming one with a fully enslaved population, which is what we see today.

While we may have "freedom of speech," we certainly do not possess true liberty of expression; go too far outside what the Jesuits deem "acceptable," and you wind up publicly shamed, broke, imprisoned or dead.

America's Shadow Government: An International Corporation

A prime example: in 1871, the Jesuits formed a shadow government, an international corporation known as the United States of America, within the bounds of the District of Columbia.

To do so, the Jesuits had Congress pass "An Act To Provide A Government for the District of Columbia," which effectively nullified the original Constitution (The Constitution for the united states of America) and replaced it with a new one, THE CONSTITUTION OF THE UNITED STATES OF AMERICA. Why would an area, defined by law as a "state," need its own "constitution" with wording nearly identical to the original Constitution for the United States? Simply put, the Jesuits' corporate constitution functions in an *economic* capacity on behalf of the Jesuits.

This new constitution operates well beyond the strict bounds of our original Constitution by stripping us of all the rights so granted and replacing them with "relative" rights or privileges. Since 1871, Americans have been living under this privately owned shadow government of the Jesuits, although Americans have been led to believe the original organic Constitution still exists to protect its citizens.

Remember, those who serve this shadow government and its attendant Jesuit masters are not obligated to be honest and truthful in dealings with ordinary Americans. Those who serve the corporation, i.e. all politicians and other employees of the US government, are no longer beholden to the citizens of America. In fact, those in the shadow government are encourage to lie, cheat and steal at every turn and to conceal their actions and behaviors from the American people.

When a politician lies to the American people, he is not committing a traitorous act because he is acting on behalf of the corporation, not the American public.

You should treat the American government like a typical corporation, e.g. Walmart or Microsoft: if you do not like the products or services, stop using them, do not support them, and encourage all your family and friends to follow your lead.

Americans in the 1770s would have revolted against this current malevolent Jesuit behavior, but Americans now do not because they are numbed by drugs and toxins in food, mind-controlling programming in movies, tv shows and news programs, sports and other mindless forms of entertainment, and countless other distractions that blind all to the harmful machinations of the Jesuits.

Our government today is a puppet show of epic stature and high production value, artistically created and painted in grand fashion by experts in the art of gentle manipulation and persuasion of the American and worldwide public, the vast majority of whom swallow the bait wholesale. Not only that, they beg for more.

The End Game: World Control Under One Roof
How clever the Jesuits to infiltrate and control every country on

Mother Earth, then attempt to build an even grander scheme: a mononation and single government that rules over all citizens.

There are many reasons for the creation and implementation of WWI, not the least of which was to bring all nations together—most under force—under one global rule.

Enter: the League of Nations (LN). Established in 1920, the LN was designed to prevent further wars by providing a global security force and ensuring all nations' citizens were effectively disarmed.

One need only take an hour to read the LN's charter, or covenant, to see hidden purposes. Some glaring examples:

Preamble: ". . . to ensure, by the acceptance of principles and the institution of methods, that armed force shall not be used, save in the common interest, and to employ international machinery for the promotion of the economic and social advancement of all peoples."

Historically the only measure used to effect measurable change in any country was by force and this involved soldiers and weapons of war. Given the LN mandated complete disarmament of each country's citizens, that left only one entity with the world authority to bear arms: the army of the LN.

As for employing "international machinery for the promotion of the economic and social advancement of all peoples," what person of sane mind would allow an international group to determine its economic and social evolution? We see today that people of different race and religion cannot agree on the smallest of terms, so imagine having a dispassionate observer dictating how you will conduct your business and personal interests.

Chapter V: The Security Council, Article 23: 1. The Security Council shall consist of fifteen Members of the United Nations. The Republic of China, France, the Union of Soviet Socialist Republics, the United Kingdom of Great Britain and Northern Ireland, and the United States of America shall be permanent members of the Security Council. The General Assembly shall elect ten other Members of the United Nations to be non-permanent members of the Security Council, due regard being specially paid, in the first instance to the contribution of Members of the United Nations to the maintenance of international peace and security and to the other purposes of the Organization, and also to equitable geographical distribution.

Please pay particular attention to the nations that were to be permanent members: Republic of China (now People's Republic of China), France, the Union of Soviet Socialist Republics (now Russia), the United Kingdom of Great Britain and Northern Ireland (now UK), and the United States of America.

These choices were by no means left to chance. China and Russia, even back then, were being manufactured to become world powers that would oppose the US and also serve as a manufacturing base that would eventually take over the majority of manufacturing and production jobs from the US, and ultimately plunge America into economic ruin.

For hundreds of years, the UK has been the public seat of financial power in the world, with Switzerland serving as the actual power deep behind the black curtain and far removed from public scrutiny.

The US, of course, was still being groomed to be the world leader for a certain period of time, from approximately 1945-2025, so it was imperative to have it not only as a permanent member but recognized leader.

As with many Jesuit intrigues, the LN ultimately failed on many levels and was thus scrapped. They felt they could build a more powerful and globally accepted world government, but needed a bigger spark to attract a much larger portion of the worldwide population: WWII.

By the end of The Second Great War, the citizens of the world were beaten down sufficiently to acquiesce to the Jesuits' latest offering, the United Nations (UN), whose official existence was acknowledged on 24 October 1945, only a few short months following the end of the war.

One World, One Lawful Government

Think here: such a lofty idea, the creation of a world-governing body, should have taken many years. And, in fact, it did. Decades, even.

The Jesuits planned to establish the UN shortly after it became evident that the League of Nations would not gain sufficient hold to become the world's leading governing body. Everything had been in place over the years. All that was necessary was the small matter of bringing WWII to a dramatic close.

Since its inception, the UN has secretly been the international face of the Jesuits, which have secretly ghostwritten many "international treaties and resolutions" that have subjugated the rights of citizens the world over. Although never advertised by BigMedia, various UN treaties and resolutions have stripped Americans of various rights that were previously guaranteed by the organic US Constitution.

In fact, the Jesuits are using the UN to slowly erode the Constitution so much that it is little more than a dead letter. The latest insults are aimed at disarming American citizens, with the passage of the UN Arms Trade Treaty (ATT), which takes careful aim at our Constitution's Second Amendment: Right to Bear Arms. Like all other UN issues, this one has been ongoing officially for more than 60 years, with the establishment of the UN's Disarmament Commission.

The UN now even has an entire department, United Nations Office for Disarmament Affairs (UNODA) and its Conventional Arms Branch (CAB), solely dedicated to disarming all citizens of the world.

From their website: "On 2 April 2013, the General Assembly adopted the landmark Arms Trade Treaty (ATT), regulating the international trade in conventional arms, from small arms to battle tanks, combat aircraft and warships. The treaty will foster peace and security by thwarting uncontrolled destabilizing arms flows to conflict regions. It will prevent human rights abusers and violators of the law of war from being supplied with arms. And it will help keep warlords, pirates, and gangs from acquiring these deadly tools."

While UNODA and CAB cleverly advertise ATT as targeting criminals and illegal activity, it's real purpose is to disarm Americans. After all, the greatest threat to the Jesuits is an armed citizenry: one with weapons capable of assaulting and killing their leaders and fighting their soldiers, and one with intimate knowledge about the

Jesuits and their machinations. If they can take away your weapons and keep you ignorant of their actions, then they have already won. The next step is simply to carry out their planned actions to further enslave you and reach their end game.

The UN also has passed measures that allow foreign military troops on American soil "for training purposes." What they really mean is, since our own Constitution does not allow our military to take up arms against US citizens, the UN established a way around this law, and has already secretly been implementing it for more than 30 years.

An example of how the UN will use foreign troops in America: a false-flag attack by a Jesuit organization (CIA, Mossad, Virginia Militia, or some covert unit) provokes Americans to riot. Federal and local law enforcement will be "overwhelmed" by the rioters. Officials then invoke the Canada-US Civil Assistance Plan to allow foreign troops inside US borders as "law-enforcement providers," granted with wide power to quell the riot and any further uprising by any means necessary.

One can only imagine the carnage inflicted on the American people by this foreign armed force, and the aftermath of such an act. If the trust of the American people had been on thin ice before such a movement, think of the possible repercussions. There is no longer any safety or security, only tentative peace and temporary comfort.

Consider the Jesuits' bottom line in establishing and maintaining governments all over the world: the Jesuits completely control a government, and a government completely controls its people.

Today's Average American Citizens: Lazy, Ignorant Cowards

Look around you today. What do you see? An entire planet of more than 165 individual governments, with more than 7 billion people, most of whom live in distressed physical and economic conditions, and almost none of whom say a word about it, let alone take up arms and overthrow their oppressors.

Perhaps surprising to many, Thomas Jefferson had this to say about government:

"Societies exist under three forms, sufficiently distinguishable. 1. Without government, as among our Indians. 2. Under government wherein the will of every one has a just influence; as is the case in England in a slight degree, and in our States in a great one. 3. Under government of force, as is the case in all other monarchies, and in most of the other republics.

"To have an idea of the curse of existence in these last, they must be seen. It is a government of wolves over sheep. It is a problem not clear in my mind that the first condition is not the best. But I believe it to be inconsistent with any great degree of population. The second state has a great deal of good in it ... It has its evils too, the principal of which is the turbulence to which it is subject ... But even this evil is productive of good. It prevents the degeneracy of government, and nourishes a general attention to public affairs. I hold that a little rebellion now and then is a good thing."

Jefferson wrote the following to a fellow correspondent:

"God forbid that we should ever be twenty years without such a rebellion! ... What country can preserve its liberties if its rulers are not warned from time to time that the people preserve the spirit of resistance? Let them take up arms ... The tree of liberty must be refreshed from time to time with the blood of patriots and tyrants. It is its natural manure."

Unfortunately, today's average American citizen is too preoccupied with noise and distractions to voice any opposition to the despotic American government, let alone do anything meaningful to change it for the better. Worst of all, Americans have no idea of the hidden power behind the public government.

Voltairine de Cleyre's words, written more than 100 years ago, echo loudly throughout America today:

"Even within the lifetime of the revolutionists, the spirit decayed. The love of material ease has been, in the mass of men and permanently speaking, always greater than the love of liberty. Nine hundred and ninety-nine women out of a thousand are more interested in the cut of a dress than in the independence of their sex; nine hundred and ninety-nine men out of a thousand are more interested in drinking a glass of beer than in questioning the tax that is laid on it; how many children are not willing to trade the liberty to play for the promise of a new cap or a new dress?"

How is it that the words of this brilliant thinker did not penetrate the minds of Americans a century ago?

Even then, the Jesuits' clever PR machine spun Voltairine de Cleyre as an "anarchist," a dangerous criminal who opposed "good" government and, therefore, the people under it. The free-thinking de Cleyre was branded the equivalent of a "conspiracy theorist" by the Jesuits, and was thus banished to the fringes of society, her words seemingly lost even in a mild breeze.

A similar sentiment was made by Luther Kauffman, Esq. in an address to leaders of The Methodist Episcopal Ministers' Meeting on December 12, 1921. It was later published as a small book, *Romanism As a World Power*:

"The great sin and crime of the American people is indifference to public affairs. We are all of us, so much concerned with the accumulation of wealth, or the pursuit of pleasure, that we forget the great heritage of a free government and free institutions which have been handed down to us by our patriotic fathers.

"The American people, as a whole, are very much in the position of a spendthrift, who has inherited a magnificent estate from his forefathers—an estate in which he has had no part in the accumulation thereof—but which he is neglecting and permitting to go to ruin. The beautiful palace in which he lives is going to decay; the beautiful lawn is being filled with weeds; the fences tumbling down; and a general spirit of negligence and wastefulness prevalent everywhere."

Silencing Dissent And Opposition Among The American People

Unfortunately, in today's rough climate, it is becoming more dangerous to voice one's own opinion, especially if it counters the moves of the Jesuits. In many countries, it is against the law to speak out against one's government. Doing so has condemned many to death or years in prison. France is the latest country to crack down on dissenters, effectively shuttering many popular alternative-news websites.

In America, one need only read the summary of a paper, *Conspiracy Theories*, by Cass Sunstein and Adrian Vermeule to appreciate the lengths the American government is willing to go to silence dissenters:

"Many millions of people hold conspiracy theories; they believe that powerful people have worked together in order to withhold the truth about some important practice or some terrible event. A recent example is the belief, widespread in some parts of the world, that the attacks of 9/11 were carried out not by Al Qaeda, but by Israel or the United States. Those who subscribe to conspiracy theories may create serious risks, including risks of violence, and the existence of such theories raises significant challenges for policy and law. The first challenge is to understand the mechanisms by which conspiracy theories prosper; the second challenge is to understand how such theories might be undermined. Such theories typically spread as a result of identifiable cognitive blunders, operating in conjunction with informational and reputational influences. A distinctive feature of conspiracy theories is their self-sealing quality. Conspiracy theorists are not likely to be persuaded by an attempt to dispel their theories; they may even characterize that very attempt as further proof of the conspiracy. Because those who hold conspiracy theories typically suffer from a "crippled epistemology," in accordance with which it is rational to hold such theories, the best response consists in cognitive infiltration of extremist groups. Various policy dilemmas, such as the question whether it is better for government to rebut conspiracy theories or to ignore them, are explored in this light."

William Garner Tears Apart The Sunstein/Vermeule Paper

Before the first sentence can complete itself, it gives away the trumped-up essence of the Jesuits' argument against those who would argue against their policies:

"Many millions of people hold conspiracy theories. . . ."

According to William Garner, the mere act of elevating one's personal belief to a "theory" is preposterous at best, dangerous and sinister at worst. In any sound study of science, one comes up with a question about a particular subject. He then proceeds to formulate a hypothesis that seeks not only to understand but to provide a definitive answer to his original question.

After sufficient and careful study, the researcher comes to a conclusion that either supports or refutes his hypothesis. And after more and more study and examination, perhaps this original hypothesis is further proven to be so robust that he elevates his hypothesis to the lofty and important position of "theory."

This new theory is now seen as highly significant in, and important to, that particular field of study. Proponents may not only support it openly and publicly, they may venerate it because of its extreme rank and gravity. This new theory is then published, its contents widely disseminated for all to see, admire and study further.

William Garner contends that, what makes the Sunstein/Vermeule paper so dangerous to ordinary American citizens is the fact the Jesuits have immediately elevated what should be called and universally accepted as a personal opinion or even hypothesis to the lofty and important rank of theory, artificially placing huge importance on, and calling undue attention to, that so-called "theory," and even calling it a potential danger or imminent threat to the government.

This practice is also dangerous to ordinary Americans because it immediately labels that "theorist" as a threat to the Jesuits, providing them swift recourse to pursue legal (or unlawful lethal) action against the "conspiracy theorist."

Let's consider another angle: if some ordinary person formulates a hypothesis that 9/11 was an inside job, perpetrated by the Israelis, and the government does not have in place its term "conspiracy theory" or "conspiracy theorist," then that accusation leveled by this ordinary American might be called a "crackpot idea" or "silly notion" or simply "one man's hypothesis," and be summarily dismissed by the government simply because it is only one man's belief, not one to be taken seriously.

And because it is ignored by the government, it is similarly dismissed by everyone else. After all, it was only a person's idea or hypothesis, something we Americans have every day. Who could possibly take those seriously, let alone consider them a serious threat?

However, once you take that same "hypothesis" by this ordinary American and slap on a toxic label like DANGER: CONSPIRACY THEORY, the whole situation changes from a child's game or amateur's free expression to serious combat where the Jesuits now have an "excuse" to legally pursue action against this man. And they could interpret his behavior in severe legal terms under the Patriot Act, which may automatically brand him a "domestic terrorist," one subject to immediate prosecution and imprisonment. Habeas corpus would be suspended.

Frightening as it sounds, it is indeed a clear and present threat to all members of American society, especially those who speak out against the government and the Jesuits. Any ordinary American can be labeled a terrorist and be thrown in prison without legal recourse of any kind and without any contact with his family or the outside world. Indefinitely.

As stated previously, our freedom of speech and liberty of expression are being violated on many levels. Without the liberty of openly criticizing those who rule us, a right guaranteed under our organic Constitution, we become slaves to a dictatorship.

The Jesuits' Latest Tactic Is Laughable

The Jesuits' latest tactics to diffuse attempts to publish negative information about conspiracies are clever (and laughable):

BigMedia publications are now including in their stories a section about "Conspiracy Theories." This tactic lists possible "theories" about why or how an action came about, and immediately disarms prospective reports about these conspiracies, giving those of us who report on them little room to maneuver.

Some tv shows (e.g. Hawaii Five-O) now include a character who is a so-called "conspiracy theorist."

These characters are cartoonish at best, not unlike Hawaii Five-O's Jerry Ortega, designed to train the public to see all of us who research and report on real-world conspiracies as ignorant and paranoid fools and misfits, certainly not deserving of Americans' time and effort.

In Hawaii Five-O, the stars all poke fun at various "conspiracy theories" some of which are, in fact, accurate. In the hugely popular series, which runs a whopping 20+ episodes each season, the light background music, setting, and likable characters appear to serve as "worldwide subject-matter experts on conspiracies" to an unsuspecting television audience who takes it all as fact.

The tv show The Blacklist includes specific references to "conspiracy theories," e.g. the Protocols of the Learned Elders of Zion (a Jesuit invention that has been used in different forms over 200 years). The Blacklist is a showcase for dozens of "conspiracy theories" that are each "debunked" by characters on the show. The tv shows Intelligence, The Player and Limitless also feature similar subjects and themes on "conspiracy theories."

The result is that millions of gullible Americans believe the content of these tv shows and other forms of entertainment.

People like me will continue to do good research and report on various actual conspiracies, regardless of how the Jesuits attempt to discredit us and disarm our published works.

"The truth, crushed to earth, shall rise again." [William Cullen Bryant]

History Repeats Itself On A Grand Scale

This same dangerous practice has been used in the past, although not using the same term, "conspiracy theory."

On May 21, 1792, Jesuit-controlled King George III issued a dangerous proclamation that sought not only to counter "seditious writings" against the royal crown, but to develop an information log about all accused persons and those "aiding and abetting" them.

While the King did not openly threaten any of "our faithful and loving subjects," it was understood that anyone accused of such "seditious writing" would have his head separated from his body. And that was after being hanged until barely conscious, then thrown on a rack to be chopped up slowly.

In the words of King George III:

"Whereas diverse wicked and seditious writings have been printed, published, and industriously dispersed, tending to excite tumult and disorder, by raising groundless jealousies and discontents in the minds of our faithful and loving subjects, respecting the laws and happy constitution of our government, civil and religious, established in this kingdom; and endeavoring to vilify and bring into contempt the wise and wholesome provisions made at the time of the glorious revolution, and since strengthened and confirmed by subsequent laws, for the preservation and security of the rights and liberties of our faithful and loving subjects; and whereas, diverse writings have also been printed, published, and industriously dispersed, recommending the said wicked and seditious publications to the attention of all our faithful and loving subjects; and whereas, we have also reason to believe, that correspondences have been entered into with sundry persons in foreign parts, with a view to forward the criminal and wicked purposes above-mentioned; and whereas, the wealth, happiness and prosperity of this kingdom do, under Divine Providence, chiefly depend upon a due submission to the laws, a just confidence in the integrity and wisdom of Parliament, and a continuance to the zealous attachment to the government and constitution of the kingdom, which has ever prevailed in the minds of the people thereof; and whereas, there is nothing which we so earnestly desire, as to secure the public peace and prosperity, and to preserve to all our loving subjects the full enjoyment of their rights and liberties, both religious and civil; We, therefore, being resolved, as far as in us lies, to repress the wicked and seditious practices aforesaid, and to deter all persons from following so pernicious an example, have thought fit, by the advice of our privy counsel, to issue this our royal proclamation, solemnly warning all our loving subjects, as they tender their own happiness, and that of their posterity, to guard against all such attempts, which aim at the subversion of all regular government within this kingdom, and which are inconsistent with the peace and order of society; and earnestly exhorting them at all times, and to the utmost of their power, to avoid and discourage all proceedings, tending to produce riots and tumults; and we do strictly charge and command all our magistrates in and throughout our kingdom of Great Britain, that they do, in their several and respective stations, take the most immediate and effectual care to suppress and prevent all riots, tumults, and other disorders, which may be attempted to be raised or made by any person or persons, which, on whatever protects they are grounded, are not only contrary to law, but dangerous to the most important interests of the kingdom; and we do further require and command all and every one of our magistrates aforesaid, that they do, from time to time, transmit to one of our principal secretaries of state, due and full information about such persons as shall be found offending aforesaid, or in any degree aiding or abetting therein; it being our determination, for the preservation of the peace and happiness of our faithful and loving subjects, to carry the laws vigorously into execution against such offenders as aforesaid.

Given at our Court at the Queen's-house, the 21st day of May, 1792, in the thirty-second year of our reign.

God save the King."

Constitutional Republic Vs. Democracy

Today the word democracy is immediately mentioned when referring to America. I hear people proudly say, "We're so fortunate to live in a democracy!"

Today, we have many organizations that seek to restore this so-called democracy: "Democracy Awakening" by the People for the American Way, "Democracy Spring," a historic grassroots sit-in and mobilization of citizens in Washington DC, the "Democracy Initiative" that seeks to restore the core principals of political equality, and the television show "Democracy Now."

A noble gesture, or clever means to undermine whatever form of government the American people are currently living under?

Aren't we living in a republic, as stated in The Pledge of Allegiance, and bound by the organic Constitution?

When did we become a democracy?

The US Pledge of Allegiance: "I pledge allegiance to the flag of the United States of America, and to the Republic for which it stands, one Nation under God, indivisible, with liberty and justice for all."

In our pledge, you clearly see the words republic and liberty, but not democracy.

Reading over the definitions of the words republic and democracy, you don't see major differences at first as they both involve citizens being active in the process. But after careful analysis, what stands out within these definitions is that underlying a republic and constitution are laws and the power of the citizens having a voice in voting in these laws.

But a democracy speaks of a rule of majority without explicitly mentioning anything about a rule of law. In addition, power is exercised either directly or indirectly through representation of the majority.

How do we arrive at a majority? What rules, if any, are in place to prevent representatives from influencing citizens to create a majority for a specific agenda that will not ultimately benefit American citizens?

The differences are subtle but significant in the grand scheme of things.

A republic is decentralized and representative of the people. Government's purpose is strictly limited by the Constitution to the protection of liberty and private property ownership.

A democracy, on the other hand, demands centralized power, controlled by majority opinion without regard to individual rights or protection of private property. Democracy subverts liberty and undermines prosperity.

It's now obvious that the goals of a democracy and a constitutional republic are incongruent.

At the close of the Constitutional Convention of 1787, Benjamin Franklin was queried as he left Independence Hall on the final day of deliberation. In the notes of Dr. James McHenry, one of Maryland's delegates to the Convention, a lady named Mrs. Powell of Philadelphia asked Dr. Franklin, "Well, Doctor, what have we got, a republic or a monarchy."

Without hesitation, Franklin replied, "A republic . . . if you can keep it."

The Founding Fathers clearly understood the dangers of a democracy. One of the architects of the Constitution, Madison, was fearful of the established histories of past democracies:

"Democracies have ever been the spectacles of turbulence and contention; have ever been found incompatible with personal security or the rights of property; and have in general been as short in their lives as they have been violent in their death."

> Today, anyone expressing concern for their personal liberty is condemned for being self-centered and selfish and for their lack of patriotism and not supporting the needs of the majority.

Edmund Randolph of Virginia echoed Madison's fears in his statement, "The general object was to produce a cure for the evils under which the United States labored; that in tracing these evils to their origins, every man had found it in the turbulence and follies of democracy."

These strongly held views about the evils of democracy and the benefits of a Constitutional Republic were shared by all of the Founding Fathers, even though some were being directed by the Jesuits from Rome. They also understood that a constitution in and by itself did not guarantee liberty in a republican form of government.

The best constitution is only as good as the moral standards and desires of the people. Without moral standards, the Constitution is basically a useless piece of paper with good intentions. The prime goal and concern of some of the Founding Fathers was liberty, while those who were clearly Jesuit-controlled pushed for a despotic democracy.

If certain Founding Fathers were alive today, they would be dismayed to see that we have allowed our once proud republic to decay over time and, with Jesuit coercion, morph into a democracy. The gradual erosion of liberty went unnoticed and although the republic was designed to protect the minority against the dictates of the majority, today we find the opposite is true.

What Then Has This Jesuit-Inspired Democracy Brought Us?

The illegal federal income tax; bloated and inefficient welfare programs; special-interest groups that have established themselves through majority rule; outside interventions in the affairs of other nations without their consent; the need for an international police force via the UN, moving us in the direction of a one-world government; humanitarianism with seemingly good intentions that actually promotes violence and displaces other cultures through population transfer, resettlement and ethnic cleansing; fractional-reserve banking that creates increasing debt through a private financial system controlled by a powerful elite minority; international policies that suppress individual liberties and the protection of private property; declining moral standards and a lack of personal responsibility by citizens, to name a few.

Are you sure you want to live in a democracy?

We've all been duped by the Jesuits and their minions through the machinations of a hidden hand working behind the scenes for many decades. This slow, methodical and insidious transition from a constitutional republic to a democracy now marching toward fascism, was their plan all along. The evidence is overwhelming. Their crowning achievement will be a one-world government, thanks in large part to millions of lazy, ignorant cowards.

The creation of the 1913 Federal Reserve Act and the implementation of a private centralized banking system pushed America further toward democracy.

Within this system, all chartered banks in the United States had to become members of and purchase specified non-transferable stock in their regional Federal Reserve banks and to set aside a stipulated amount of non-interest bearing reserves with their respective banks.

Our governmental banking system was now fully and legally in the hands of a group of private elite taking orders from the Jesuits who had the ability to destabilize the economy at will through speculation, inflation and false-flag events like 9/11 and planned stock market crashes.

Further fuel was the passing of the 16th Amendment, also known as the US Personal Income Tax. Coincidentally, this also occurred in 1913.

It read, "The Congress shall have power to lay and collect taxes on incomes, from whatever source derived, without apportionment among the several States, and without regard to any census or enumeration."

Without regard to any census or enumeration? How do these words strike you? In sum, they are illegal at best, destructive to all Americans at worst. They allow the Jesuits to levy a personal income tax without reasonable restrictions.

The personal income tax is illegal because it was never properly ratified, plus the final text of the act differed from what Congress had originally proposed. Most members of Congress had gone home for the holidays and there weren't enough members to legally ratify this amendment.

This same underhanded method was used by President Bush to get the Patriot Act signed. The few Congress members who were allowed to read the bloated Patriot Act were only given one week to read this document that exceeded 1,000 pages.

Democracy's main component is the concept of "majority rule," through which democracy can flourish. The majority is assumed to be in charge today and can do whatever is pleases. If the majority has not yet sanctioned some desired egregious action demanded by special interests, the propaganda machine goes into operation, and the pollsters relay the results back to the politicians who are seeking legitimacy in their endeavors.

Recall how the Jesuits built America by flooding it with subservient Roman Catholics who served as a "majority" on many legal and social issues of the day. In effect, the "majority" was a wholly manufactured entity.

The rule of law and the Constitution have become irrelevant. We live by constant polls. This trend toward authoritarian democracy was tolerated because it was done in the name of benevolence, fairness and equity for all. Directed by the Jesuits, the pretense of love and compassion by those who desire to remold society and undermine the Constitution convinced the recipients, and even the victims, of its necessity.

Special-interest groups, usually aimed at helping the poor, form coalitions that ban together for the common good, form a majority and then vote things for themselves and expect others to provide for them with hesitating or questioning. Then they convince the government to fund these benevolent projects with good intentions.

The government is inefficient and rarely achieves its goals via the special interest groups that personally benefit, perpetuating the need for those inefficient, bulky and inflated programs to exist.

Democracy is the most expensive form of government.

To make matters worse, wealthy elites benefit from this unaccountable system by skimming money off the top, a practice that rarely gets noticed. It's a vicious cycle of money being funneled into a spiraling, out-of-control cost structure for programs that will eventually fail when the money runs out.

This system works against the original goal of helping those in need, those truly disadvantaged. Greed and power triumph over charity. This is one aspect of the welfare state that democracy promotes.

For the benefits to continue, politicians must reject the rule of law and concern themselves only with the control of majority opinion. The politicians are directed by the Jesuits so the rule of law is irrelevant as they find ways to get around it.

Once a nation shifts toward becoming a democracy, the rule of government changes dramatically. Instead of government's role being that of guaranteeing liberty, equality under the law and protection of private property, it shifts its focus away from individuals and embarks on the impossible task of achieving economic equality (redistribution of the nation's wealth), micro-managing the economy and protecting citizens from themselves and what they are allowed to do with their own property.

Then, for the government to carry out its new duties, power must now be transferred from the citizens to the politicians, who are hand-chosen by the Jesuits for a specific agenda.

And that's where we are today, with citizens competing with one another to get our politicians to serve their specific interests. They want their piece of the financial handouts they see others receiving without regard to the long-term consequences. It becomes a vicious cycle of never-ending spending.

Spending is predictable in a democracy: it always increases.

Now, power and public opinion become the determining factors in directing government funding through the use of Jesuit propaganda, demagoguery and control of the education system.

The Jesuit-controlled Rothschild family financial banking system is currently strangling us, thanks to our democracy. Borrowing and central bank credit creation are generally used, because they are less noticeable but more deceitful than direct taxation, which would amount to pay-as-you-go.

Even with an income tax, the planners for welfare and warfare knew it would become necessary to eliminate the restraints on printing money. Private counterfeiting was a heinous crime, but government counterfeit and fractional-reserve banking were required to seductively pay for the majority's demands.

It is for this reason that democracies always bring about currency debasement through inflation and sometimes hyperinflation of the money supply.

If direct taxation were accomplished through monthly checks written by each taxpayer, the cost of government would be quickly revealed and this democratic con-game would end much more quickly.

Passing on debt to the next generation through borrowing is also a popular way to pay for warfare and welfare, the "guns and butter" philosophy.

Like our social welfarism at home, our foreign meddling and empire-building abroad are a consequence of our becoming a pure democracy. Democracy overseas leads to empire-building, and we justify our interventions with a tone of moral arrogance; after all, if it's good for Americans, it's good for everyone else.

This occurs without regard for the rule of law a republic demands. Instead of following the Constitution and rule of law, we allow the Jesuit-controlled media and its propaganda machine to take us to war, based on majority opinion by manipulating its citizens and then deferring to the UN for its seal of approval, thus usurping the Constitution and one of its prime intended purposes.

Those nations that hold the rein of power can dictate the perceived will of the people, allowing those same nations to control UN policies abroad. Bribery, threats and intimidation are common practices used to achieve a "democratic" consensus, regardless of the perceived benefits to other nations. The Vatican (read: the Jesuits) have perfected the practice of manipulating countries that disagree with their way of thinking.

Humanitarianism under a democracy usually involves violence, especially when it involves the UN. Today we see it in regions where "humanitarian efforts" are being carried out in earnest: many parts of Africa, for example. The greater the human outreach, the greater the violence to achieve it.

Each act of inhumanity by the government undermines the essential element of human progress: individual liberty. And then an impassioned appeal to patriotism is used to convince people that a little sacrifice of liberty here and there is a small price to pay. The results, though, are frightening and prove just the opposite.

Benjamin Franklin: "They that can give up essential liberty to obtain a little temporary safety deserve neither safety nor liberty."

Some of the damage to liberty and the Constitution is done by ignorant men and women of good will who are convinced they know what is best for the economy, for others and foreign powers. They fail to recognize their arrogance in assuming they know what is best and just how ignorant about their Jesuit rulers they truly are.

C.S. Lewis wrote, in *God in the Dock: Essays on Theology*, "Of all tyrannies, a tyranny sincerely exercised for the good of its victims may be the most oppressive. It would be better to live under robber barons than under omnipotent moral busybodies. The robber baron's cruelty may sometimes sleep, his cupidity may at some point be satiated; but those who torment us for our own good will torment us without end for they do so with the approval of their own conscience."

Even though the vast majority of Americans have been indoctrinated and manipulated to believe that democracy is a favorable system, know that the goals of pure democracy and that of a constitutional republic are incompatible.

One of the prime advantages of a republic is that liberty releases creative energy while government intervention suppresses it. This release of creative energy was never greater than in the time following the American Revolution and the writing of the organic US Constitution.

In a republic, freedom requires self-control and moral responsibility. Without these key ingredients, prosperity for the masses is impossible and as a nation we become vulnerable to outside threats. In a republic, the people are in charge. The Constitution provides strict restraints on the politicians, bureaucrats and the military. Everything the government is allowed to do is only done with explicit permission from the people or the Constitution.

Today it's directly the opposite as we move toward tyranny and fascism, just what the Jesuits had planned all along. Under democracy and fascism, the pseudo-capitalists write the laws that undermine the Constitution and jeopardize the rights and property of all Americans.

When the government assumes responsibility for individuals, it does so at the expense of liberty and then must resort to force and intimidation. Freedom of choice is gone. The government then dictates to its citizens what one can eat, drink or smoke, all basic freedoms guaranteed under the organic Constitution. We have already entered this chilling phase of this debilitating democracy.

The Constitution wasn't perfect and neither were the true loyal Founding Fathers, but their underlying intentions were pure, even though some were under the secret control of the Jesuits. The Founding Fathers already knew about the concept of a democracy, its track record of failure throughout history and the turbulent and contentious aspects that lead to the violent deaths of all prior democracies.

A republic was, and still is, the best choice for our nation. Our greatest hope is that there is still time to restore our republic and for the organic Constitution to be revered and followed as the basis of law once again.

Sadly, this dream is in direct contrast to the Jesuits' long-term plan to establish a one-world government and subjugate of the rights of all good Americans.

Freedom And Liberty: The Difference Can Kill You

The subjugation of Americans' freedom and liberty has been ongoing since America's founding.

But what is freedom, really? And how does it differ from liberty?

William Garner said:

"Freedom is merely a two-dimension concept of independence, something written on paper. It's like having a million bucks in the bank and never spending it. But liberty is something quite different and significant: liberty is freedom in motion, actually spending that million dollars."

Look all around you, study history over decades and centuries and clear and distinct patterns of behavior and action will emerge: the Jesuits have slowly and stealthily subjugated the rights and liberties of American citizens. You are now living under a shadow government that exerts dangerous control, and this insidious cloak is well disguised by all the noise and distractions of family, work, health, play time, BigEntertainment, BigSports, etc.

In addition to being distracted, you are chemically numbed by demoralizing and depressing news and information that continually bombards you each day.

The only possible relief you can hope to get comes from educating yourself about the system that controls you and your liberty, your rights. Only then can you begin to appreciate how serious this situation really is, and make changes in your life to counter it.

For those of you who ask, "When does the world collapse?"

In a few thousand years, probably.

Since the false-flag attacks in September of 2001, the Jesuits have greatly accelerated their malevolent actions against our beloved America. Perhaps you'll begin to see and feel some of them, if you are not too numb or distracted.

If you feel nothing at all, maybe it's best for you and your family.

After all, sheer ignorance often shelters us from disaster.

2

American Politics: The Grand Lie

"Jesuit math: 1/2 truth + 1/2 truth = The Whole Truth."
—William Garner

In the early 17th century, the Old World of Europe was becoming stale and unproductive, her workers and toilers growing uneasy with continued monarchical rule that favored the ruling elite and did little if anything useful for the working class and poor, which were more difficult to manipulate and control.

England appeared to be largely Protestant on the outside, with Queen Elizabeth I openly despising Catholicism and its Jesuit soldiers; the latter drove many Catholics from her shores to the New World.

The actual power behind the Tudor throne, Secretary of State William Cecil, and the Stuart throne, later his prime-minister son Robert Cecil, didn't care one way or the other what the ruling religion was, as long as their agendas were adhered to and goals met. Despite their indifference, their reigns remained anti-Catholic.

The Jesuits Build The United States Of America

The Jesuits set their sights on the New World and began designing a new form of government, one that would, on the public surface, appear to grant freedom and liberty (on paper, at least) to its citizens with the secret intent of creating a slave state of dutiful taxpayers and obedient workers. News of this new form of government and rule spread across Europe and attracted some of the brightest minds, who emigrated to the New World in search of prosperity, freedom of religion, and freedom of speech, among various other promises of independence.

Underneath the gloss, though, the Jesuits operated behind the black curtain, creating a powerful and most-secret dictatorship that rules much the same even today. Those very bright immigrants soon learned the true nature of the Jesuits and their actions in America. Some chose to leave and not bear the burden of clashing with this powerful society, others chose to remain in America and learn how to work within the new system, despotic as it was to become.

In creating the illusion of such a paradise, the Jesuits had to establish a strong government of men who were strongly opposed to monarchical rule on every level and who were vehemently hostile to any rule whatsoever by the Vatican and its despotic Roman Catholic Church. So the Jesuits developed various schemes to fool, entice and coerce many future leaders of America to emigrate to the New World and help build the Jesuits' vision of this new sham government. These men had come from England and France, where liberties even to many of the non-aristocratic elite were few.

To appreciate the full picture of the Jesuits' new scheme, please consider this: if you had a high-value asset like the early American government, which, on its surface, represented the world's first platform of true liberty, with elected leaders and unheard-of freedoms, would you dare leave it in the hands of ordinary men to run, i.e., those not in your complete control? Could you actually trust anyone on that extreme level with your grand prize?

Of course not.

Which is why the Jesuits carefully chose their minions to fill certain stations within this new federal government and system of state governments, groomed future leaders from the ranks of Europe's ruling elite, and attracted other future leaders from the ordinary population, trained them according to their high standards, and retained only the most promising ones for various leadership roles.

As the Jesuits designed the new American government, they took a page from the playbooks of old: set up a system of built-in antagonism. Then divide and conquer. The Jesuits did not invent this method of control and manipulation, but they certainly have perfected it over the nearly 500 years they have been in power.

Take a population, slice into two parts, control each part by pitting the two groups against each other in many ways, so members of the two parts see each other as mortal enemies. Repeat as necessary until you achieve the desired result, which is subjugation of the entire population. It has worked well in every single country the Jesuits have conquered, when they were unable to control an entire population as a whole.

This tactic also works well against those specific sectors of a given population (people of a particular belief, for example) that the Jesuits wish to attract and control. The Jesuits identify their targets, design and institute a new "attractant," which may be a political party or some form of entertainment, hook their desired catch, and simply pull them in. Those who comply are rewarded. Dissenters are banished to the margins.

Fifty years ago, the political landscape was seen publicly as a gentlemen's game: politicians who acted and looked the part, little rhetoric or personal attacks in the media, few publicly leaked scandals, toned-down presentations of any political affairs on tv.

The 1950s and '60s were a quieter time in politics for the American public, because the Jesuits were still building the government's infrastructure after WWII and instituting new departments to fit the prevailing climate and also to prepare for coming ones.

Television was a relatively new tool on the stage and, like the actors themselves, was being groomed for a much grander purpose:

to unleash a new propaganda machine. For now, though, it was used by button-down reporters in dark suits, no smiles, deep commanding voices who reported on "serious" issues like the Vietnam War, anti-war protests by college kids at home, drugs and the hippie generation of do-nothings and misfits who smartly tuned out to all the goings-on. Most Americans still could not afford a television set, so the majority tuned in to radio news, shows and advertisements.

At that time, America seemed perfectly content having just two major political parties, Democratic and Republican, with a handful of minor ones that were too small and insignificant for the Jesuits to be concerned with. The Jesuits felt they could control American political sentiment and action via these two main mechanisms, which had worked well over the previous 50 years.

The Jesuits Conquer And Rule From Within

The Jesuits almost always rule from within: they start an organization via their faithful controlled followers or infiltrate an already established one whose leadership they either install or, if already in place, control via any means necessary, including bribery, extortion, kidnapping and murder of family members and close associates. This method has worked for hundreds of years across the world, and is still in wide use today. When any important Jesuit issue is threatened, they find some clever means to convince Americans to vote in favor of the Jesuits' preference.

Their method was deceptively simple: as stated previously, divide a population into two main parties, control them from within, and keep them at odds with each other by designing each with different political, social and moral ideals. The two main parties' ideals were thought to represent those of the American people at that time, and it worked well for decades until the American people began questioning their political leaders and the very system they had believed in all their lives, and we began to see the first big cracks appears in the late 1960s.

The Jesuits steered American politics in any direction they chose. Since they controlled our government and its puppet politicians, they also controlled the economy and all markets and were able to create highly effective economic depressions when they chose, or according to the points in cycles of celestiophysics, thus bringing the American people to their knees on a whim.

Being fluid in design and movement, and always evolving, the Jesuits over the years have reacted to the increased American people's distaste for either political party and so designed a third party they could use to control the new breakaway group of malcontents. In the 1970s, the Libertarian Party was instituted and, as with all other parties, controlled from within the organization.

While the Libertarians never posed any major threat to Democrats or Republicans, they were successful in bringing together hundreds of thousands of those "malcontents" who may otherwise have somehow disrupted the political system, even at a state or local level. With so much to lose, the Jesuits were not willing to leave it to chance, so they instituted that safety valve.

Any major political party is used by the Jesuits to control a large portion of the American population, because it represents virtually every important issue affecting Americans, from political to economic to social to education to military. What this party does not control, other organizations, even non-governmental ones like Hollywood and BigEntertainment, BigMusic, BigPharma, certainly do, using a billion-dollar PR machine that has made even the worst and most detrimental policies look completely disarming.

Witness: the tobacco industry's fight to manufacture poisonous cigarettes and cigars; the pharmaceutical industry's fight to manufacture harmful drugs, test them in Third World countries on an unsuspecting population, then unleash them on another ignorant population, the American people; the chemical industry's fight to manufacture harmful substances without regard for the safety and health of Americans.

Today's political landscape is far from its cousin only 50 years ago: politicians no longer look and act the part; they are cartoon characters. Rhetoric and personal attacks are at an all-time high, and are being carried out openly in the media, where deeply personal issues are brought to the front, like so many dramas on popular soap operas and telenovellas. Scandals abound like never before and are celebrated as big events by BigMedia- and BigEntertainment-loving Americans.

The entire political arena is a laughable circus act, carefully scripted and choreographed by multi-million-dollar production companies and PR firms that create brilliant illusion and spin.

But, unlike a carnival show, this one is highly effective at attracting more and more Americans to its performances, and enticing them to do the bidding of the Jesuits. All one need do is examine one of the results: Americans' public anti-political sentiment and actions are at an all-time high. So instead of bashing American politics, political parties and candidates, Americans have been pulled away to a new distraction and are now mesmerized by some dazzling form of entertainment. Hours a day. Three hundred and sixty-five days a year. All you can eat.

The Jesuits have evolved well: when politics failed to control the population, they simply designed and introduced new forms that would attract Americans and control their actions and behaviors.

On the outside, the formula is simple. And deadly effective on all levels. Again, one only need look at the results to affirm my points.

From its inception, the American political system has been controlled and run by the Jesuits, who have steered politics in any way they wished. As Americans became more educated, they wanted to learn how to have a hand in the decisions that affected their lives, so they got involved in that process, if only at a local level.

How An American President Is Chosen

Donald Trump was not elected President of the United States of America. He was carefully chosen by the Jesuits many years ago to fulfill a specific role that would deeply divide America, even more so than a homosexual president and his transgender wife.

During the run-up to voting day, both candidates appeared to be the least-fit of any potential candidate for the US presidency in more than 250 years. Every single American I spoke with during the weeks prior to November 8, 2016 shared the same sentiment as one elderly woman: "They both look like clowns at a three-ring circus. Who could possibly vote for such cheap trash?"

This is what the Jesuits have created in American politics: cheap and tasteless entertainment for the controlled masses.

In Europe during the inception of America, only the elite could vote. In America, nearly every man, regardless of his station, could vote. Not only this, since voting for the candidates of their choice was such a novel idea, never before seen in modern politics anywhere in the world, many of these farmers, merchants, fishermen, etc. took great interest in the political activities of their villages, towns and cities. These hard-working souls learned to vote for people who claimed to have similar values and morals, so those representatives would effectively stand for their own interests. It was a dream come true.

What those good trusting Americans did not realize then is that their representatives did not actually stand for anything other than a hook and line to attract and reel in new recruits that were soon under the control of men thousands of miles away.

Author J. Wayne Laurens, in his 1855 book, *The Crisis: or, the Enemies of America Unmasked*, wrote:

"An American gentleman was passenger on board a merchant ship, bound from London to Rio Janeiro. There were among the passengers Englishmen, Germans, Frenchmen, Spaniards, and Portuguese; but the person we refer to was the only American. Between himself and the English gentlemen, there were frequent discussions about politics, to which such of the other passengers, as could speak English, would listen, sometimes taking a part.

"Of course, our American was a great friend to the institutions of his own country; and defended republican forms of government, freedom of the speech and of the press, the vote by ballot, and all the other elements of popular sovereignty through thick and thin.

"Assailed on every side, he found his office of champion of freedom no sinecure. Every calm morning and every pleasant evening witnessed a new controversy on the deck or in the cabin; but he manfully held his ground against a host of adversaries; and being fluent in speech, strong in argument, skilled in logic, and full of lively and sarcastic humor, he generally came out of the debate with honor, taking care always to terminate the action at precisely the right moment, and to quit the field with flying colors.

"Among the persons who listened with the greatest attention to these debates, was a lean bilious looking old Frenchman, who always took care to be present, and who showed by his look and manner, that he was deeply interested in politics, although he never by any chance uttered an opinion or made a remark on political subjects, in the general circle of the passengers.

"In point of fact, this man was a Roman Catholic priest, a Jesuit of high standing, who was going to some station in South America, in obedience to an order from his superior. He was a cosmopolite indeed.

"Though not much past the middle point of life, he was rather aged in appearance, in consequence of the great variety and extent of the missions which he had performed in all quarters of the world, and in every kind of climate. From Canada to Calcutta; from the breezy heights of the Andes to the unwholesome marshes of Java, by sea and by land, in season and out of season, this man had journeyed on the secret errands of his order. Speaking fluently a dozen different languages, and possessing the most perfect power of dissimulation, as well as the most thorough devotedness to the church, and those carefully trained habits of obedience, which are so essential to the character of an able and faithful Jesuit, he had at length become one of the most accomplished men of his age.

"As he listened to the conversation of the American passenger, he could not help noticing, that he was gradually making converts to republican views. Many of these passengers, he observed, sought private interviews with the American; and by careful eavesdropping, he ascertained that their object was to ask questions about his country, and gain information respecting the actual working of the American attempt at self-government.

"When the passage was nearly over, the Frenchman happening to be alone with the American, in a retired part of the deck, where their conversation could not be overheard, commenced a quiet chat with him. Addressing him in English, which he spoke with ease and precision, he thanked him with apparent cordiality, for the entertainment he had derived from his conversation or rather eloquent haranguing to the other passengers, during the voyage.

"He professed to have enjoyed their debates very greatly; and gave the American due credit for his wit, his logic, his humour, his address, and his unbounded good nature.

"The American was much pleased at his compliments; for he had conceived a great respect for this silent and attentive auditor; and, in fact, had, in his own secret mind, set him down as a hopeful convert to Americanism; he thanked him, therefore, with much feeling, for his good opinion; at the same time disclaiming any merit, for success in defending a truth so self-evident, as that which is expressed in these few words—that a nation ought to govern itself, and that by the popular vote of its own citizens.

" 'This,' said the Jesuit, with a quiet smile, 'you suppose to be the system of your own country?'

" 'I do not suppose it,' said the American, 'I know it.'

" 'Now,' said the Jesuit, 'listen to me a few moments and I will tell you what I know. Your president is elected by the conclave of cardinals at Rome, the same who elect the pope. Your people nominate the candidates. Our confidential agents select from the number, the one whom they believe to be the most favorable to the interests of the church. His name with those of the other candidates is reported to the cardinals and the pope. When their decision is announced to the confidential friends of the pope and the cardinals, in the United States, they send forth their orders through the priests; and the whole Roman Catholic vote is thrown for the candidate who is favoured by the church. He, of course, is always elected. Your parties are so equally divided on politics, that this Roman Catholic vote, which is cast on purely religious considerations, is always sufficient to turn the scale.'

"The American looked rather blank at this announcement."

Even today, very few people understand that their political system is a complete sham, and that any representatives of theirs are chosen not by them but by people who have a specific agenda counter to their own. How could this come about without the American people knowing about it, let alone understanding such Jesuit intrigue?

BigMedia And BigEntertainment Influence The Population

BigMedia is the megaphone of the Jesuits. It is the means by which they disseminate news to the American people. News about politics and their politicians. News about healthcare and their health. News about education of their children. Any news whatsoever is constructed by the Jesuits, presented in a very slick production by pretty people you can't help but ogle and drool over.

The average American can be led about quite easily, as evidenced by the latest statistics on how often Americans watch various forms of news and especially entertainment on tv: more than five hours a day, depending on age and ethnic group.

Imagine this: you are glued to the tv for hours at a time, watching mindless entertainment or manufactured news. How much of this information do you think you will absorb? One answer comes from sociological and psychological studies on what people tend to talk about in everyday conversations:

Poor people talk about characters in tv shows, the lottery, and how to get rich quick. They do not talk of wishes and dreams, how to attain meaningful goals, how to get educated and get a great job.

Poor people also gamble much more than any other economic group. They eat more junk food than any other group. They do more illegal drugs and abuse alcohol than any other group.

And poor people watch more tv than any other group.

Interestingly, poor people over the past 50 years have had a new neighbor introduced to their lowly society: the Middle-Class American. Now, more than ever, the poor class is swelling to consume close to half of the American population. The Jesuits have nearly concluded their take-over of the American people, not just via politics but also by many other means that attract, hook and pull in unsuspecting people.

Politics Is Just One Means To Control America

And that is its primary purpose: control you and your thoughts and behaviors, regardless of which candidate you vote for, what your stance is on certain policies and issues. Today's political landscape is tightly controlled by the Jesuits and the hundreds of top-tier corporations whose CEOs do their bidding and ensure their business runs according to the playbook designed and implemented by the Jesuits.

The average voter thinks he has a say in political issues because he takes the time to vote, donates to his favorite political candidate, and supports his party any way he can.

That notion could not be further from the truth.

Policies are decided not by popular vote but by predetermined actions and outcomes behind the scenes. And they have absolutely nothing to do with the average American, except that they steer him in the direction they wish for him at that time.

Since its inception, America and her politics have been designed and controlled and manipulated by the most prolific society in modern history. They are the finest ghostwriters of both secret and public works of law that work behind the scenes, of public policies that affect everyone, of popular books that influence millions of various ages. These men are the most persuasive recruits of world-class talent they use to create works of art that manipulate the minds and souls of the population: plays, movies, stories, paintings, etc.

The members of this highly successful society are worker bees and ants, never taking credit for their own work, but rather allowing some public figure to accept the credit because the Jesuits know the public will be drawn to a likable, charismatic and beautiful public personality. They also know this: that public person can be controlled and manipulated against their will to do their bidding.

The Jesuits Control By Murder, Fear And Intrigue

American politics follows these patterns exactly, with controlled and manipulated politicians following prepared scripts written by the Jesuits. Those men and women who obey the rules are rewarded with long careers in politics or, even when they leave politics in total disgrace, in the private sector. Those unlucky few politicians who depart from the Jesuits' script or who stray too far from their party's politics are removed from office either through embarrassing scandal, threats or murder.

President William Henry Harrison served only 32 days in office as president, from March 4 to April 4, 1841, before the Jesuits poisoned him. As a message to all others who would oppose their authority, the Jesuits also brutally murdered all but one of President Harrison's family, leaving a son, John Scott Harrison, Esq., a member of Congress from Ohio, to carry the message to would-be dissenters in the future. Curiously, Congress granted the president's heirs (ultimately, only John Harrison) $25,000 in compensation for their loss, although the bill supporting it was hotly contested by parties on both sides.

In 1865, after lengthy and involved preparation, the Jesuits murdered President Abraham Lincoln, using a complex system of spies, conspirators and co-conspirators in several different countries: Canada, Mexico, America, Austria and Italy. Lincoln knew of the assassination attempt, having been informed by close friends, including Reverend Charles Chiniquy, the priest he defended against the Jesuits years before. Lincoln said this about the Jesuits:

"The Jesuits are so expert in their deeds of blood, that Henry IV said it was impossible to escape them, and he became their victim, though he did all he could to protect himself. My escape from their hands, since the letter of the Pope to Jeff. Davis has sharpened a million of daggers, is more than a miracle."

Lincoln's assassin, John Wilkes Booth, not only escaped prosecution, he lived to old age under assumed names (David E. George and John St. Helen, among others). Booth died on January 13, 1903 in Enid, in the Oklahoma Territory, after voluntarily ingesting either strychnine or arsenic.

On July 2, 1881, President James Garfield was shot and killed by Charles J. Guiteau in another well-planned Jesuit operation.

Less than six months after his election, President William McKinley was shot and killed by Jesuit assassin Leon Czolgosz, thus emplacing the highly malleable Jesuit puppet Theodore Roosevelt.

On November 22, 1963, President John F. Kennedy was gunned down by multiple assassins from the Jesuits' very own Murder, Inc., the Central Intelligence Agency (CIA), using US Army snipers who were on temporary duty to the CIA.

The list of American political assassinations by the Jesuits numbers in the hundreds and includes not only high-ranking officials of both political parties in the government, but also the White House (Deputy White House Counsel Vincent Foster), Commerce Department (Secretary Ron Brown), Defense Department (Navy Secretary James Forrestal), military (Army General George Patton, Navy Admiral Jeremy Boorda, Army Corporal Pat Tillman), Justice Department (dozens of attorneys and aids), FBI, ATF, CIA, and many other departments.

During President Clinton's presidency, more than 40 people, some close associates of the president, died suddenly under mysterious or suspicious circumstances, or were murdered outright. The probability of this many staffers and employees dying during this short period by chance alone is virtually zero.

While the vast majority of politicians since the birth of America have shrunk in terror and fear from the Jesuits, a brave few have stepped forward to warn us of the dangers. Consider what the inventor of the telegraph and Morse code had to say about the Jesuits:

"Popery [refers to the Jesuit-controlled pope and Vatican] is more dangerous and more formidable than any power in the United States, on the ground that, through its despotic organization, it can concentrate its efforts for any purpose with complete effect; and that organization being wholly under foreign control, it can have no real sympathy with anything American.

"Popery does not acknowledge the right of the people to govern, but claims for itself the supreme right to govern people and rulers by divine right. Popery does not tolerate the liberty of the press. It takes advantage, indeed, of our liberty of the press to use its own press against our liberty; but it proclaims in the thunders of the Vatican, and with a voice which it pronounces unchangeable, that it is a liberty never sufficiently to be execrated and detested.

"It does not tolerate liberty of conscience or liberty of opinion. They are denounced by the Sovereign Pontiff as a most pestilential error, a pest of all others to be dreaded in the State. It is not responsible to the people in its financial matters. It taxes at will, and is accountable to none but itself."

Sadly, more than 150 years later, even with all the warnings from keen observers and insiders and egregious Jesuit behaviors, Americans still have not gotten the message, much less understood and acted on it. This unfortunate phenomenon is a grand testament to how brilliantly the Jesuits' PR machine functions.

The Jesuits' political reign of terror continues to this day, to ensure they maintain complete control over, and manipulation of, the entire political spectrum, not to mention every sector of American society.

President Trump is but another Jesuit pawn who does his masters' bidding. Whatever his policies, you can be certain of this fact: they are the policies of the Jesuits and were designed many years ago to support a grand purpose.

3

American Religion: Chain Of Sorrows

"In Rome a tyrant and in Spain a thing
That wears a mask and bears a poisonous sting
In India a strangler, in France a knave,
In Ireland a bigot and a slave;
In our Republic a designing tool
And traitor, warring with the public school,
And whether in Greece, in Hindoostan or Spain,
His record bears the progeny of Cain...."

—Eliza Pittsinger,
excerpt from poem "The Jesuits"
in *The Black Pope* by OE Murray

According to Jmmanuel Sananda's teachings, all modern religions are false and are based on his teachings, plus the ideas and tenets of mentors who came before him, that is, extraterrestrial teachers. If he is accurate in his assertions, Jmmanuel tells us that all religions that preceded his arrival on Earth were based, in part, on the knowledge of his extraterrestrial race.

This includes the so-called Hebrew bible and any variants of it.

There is much speculation among earth-based mainstream scholars who the Hebrews and their descendants actually were and what became of them. Modern history books and texts certainly have been tainted by religious leaders, scholars and scribes who continue to uphold all laws surrounding their false religions.

Anyone studying the Jmmanuel's sermons (please see my book, *Arcanum*) and all subsequent religious texts will not be surprised to note that each text contains kernels of Jmmanuel's teachings. Modern-day bibles are bastardized versions of Jmmanuel's words, having been heavily edited to reflect the false teachings of present-day religions and their principles.

Gnosticism Vs. Roman Catholicism

Around the time just prior to Jmmanuel's arrival, the Gnostics had a very different view than the Romans. Rather than a religion, they followed their own spiritual teachings. According to John Lamb Lash in his book *Not In His Image: Gnostic Vision, Sacred Ecology and the Future of Belief*, the Gnostics, who founded and led the Mystery Schools of ancient Europe and the Near East, were accomplished mystics, inspired by a sacred theory of the earth, but they were not religious in the conventional sense. That is, they did not impose a moral code, doctrinal formulas or institutional authority.

The Gnostic message had two components: a sacred vision of the earth, and a radical critique of Salvationist doctrines centered on the Judeo-Christian messiah, especially the "redeemer complex."

The redeemer complex has four components: creation of the world by a father god, independent of a female counterpart; the trial and testing of the righteous few or "chosen people"; the mission of the creator god's son (the messiah) to save the world; and the final, apocalyptic judgment delivered by father and son upon humanity.

In layman's terms, this complex states there is inherently something wrong with us humans and that we need someone or something outside of ourselves to save us, thus the Salvationist creed.

The Gnostics wholly disagreed with this doctrine and their protests against the redeemer complex aroused an enormous wave of violence in converts to the Salvationist creed, as seen in the murder of the well-respected mathematician, astronomer and philosopher, Hypatia of Alexandria, Egypt, in the year 415 C.E.

Lash further states, "Roman Christianity adopted the larval or tribal form of the redeemer complex from Judaism, and transformed it into a universal ("catholic") program of salvation. Differing views of these four components determine various factions of Judaism and Christianity as well as Islam, which also belongs to the trinity of Abrahamic religions, although it arose after the Gnostics were silenced.

"Humans may commit violence for many reasons and they may seek to oppress and dominate others for a variety of causes, but when domination by violent force, both physical and psychological, is infused with righteousness and underwritten by "divine authority," violence takes on another dimension. It becomes inhuman and deviant.

"Like countless others of her time, Hypatia was the victim of religiously inspired sectarian violence, driven and fed by faith in the redeemer complex. What kind of world results if the power to dominate and control others, inflicting enormous suffering in the process, is sanctioned by a "divine" being who can at the same time redeem that suffering and release the perpetrators and their victims from that world's evils?

"Such was the diabolic system Gnostics found themselves facing after 150 C.E."

Roman Persecution And Genocide

There are many popular epic stories of various bibles, including Noah's flood, Sodom and Gomorrah, David and Goliath, and many others that depict abject murder and mayhem by the character known as God. In his book, *Drunk with Blood: God's Killings in the Bible*, Steve Wells includes a separate account for each of God's 158 killings. These stories fill the pages of bibles, yet are seldom read in church and are ignored by most bible believers.

In a similar vein, French statesman Baron DePonnat stated in 1940, "Roman Catholicism was born of blood, has wallowed in blood, and has quenched its thirst in blood, and it is in letters of blood that its true history is written."

Indeed, the history of Rome and her clever invention, the Roman Catholic religion, has been one of brutal torture, slaughter, mass murder, and population manipulation and control.

John Dowling, in his *History of Romanism* states, "From the birth of Popery in 606 to the present time, it is estimated by careful and credible historians that more than fifty millions of the human family have been slaughtered for the crime of heresy by popish prosecutors, an average of more than forty thousand religious murders for every year of the existence of popery."

David Plaisted states, "Surely nearly all Roman Catholics as well as Protestants disapprove of past religious persecutions, so any such discussion on this subject should not reflect negatively on current members of the Roman Catholic Church. The reason the Papacy stands out is that it has ruled for such a long period of time over such a large area, exercised so much power, and claimed divine prerogatives for its persecutions.

"The magnitude of the persecutions is important for the following reason: One can excuse a few thousand cases as exceptional, but millions and millions of victims can only be the result of a systematic policy, thereby showing the harmful results of church-state unions."

Even though the Jesuit Order wasn't formally established until 1540, they still played a huge role in murdering tens of millions of innocent people throughout the world.

In the case of the Irish Rebellion of 1641, Cushing B. Hassell states,

"In addition to the Jesuit or Catholic atrocities of this century already enumerated with some particulars, they massacred 400 Protestants at Grossoto, in Lombari, July 19th, 1620; are said to have destroyed 400,000 Protestants in Ireland, in 1641, by outright murder, and cold, and hunger, and drowning. . . ."

Dowling's estimate of 50 million humans murdered may be a very conservative estimate.

Dr. William Brownlee, in his book, *Popery An Enemy to Civil Liberty*, stated a much higher number, thanks to the Jesuits, "Why did that proud slave, Louis XIV, at the haughty pope's bidding, murder, and exile unnumbered myriads of the most industrious, and moral subjects of his own kingdom? Because he had humbled himself to become voluntarily, the pope's principal executioner, among the crowned heads of Europe, to destroy religious liberty, and the rights of conscience! Why were the horrid flames of Smithfield lighted up in England, in the Marian prosecution? Because the demon of popery, and the pope's handmaid, Queen Mary, were bent on another desperate experiment to annihilate the religious liberty of England!

"Who moved the wild Irish Catholics to massacre the Protestants of Ireland, in the first half of the 17th century? It was the pope, and his army of ferocious priests, bent on the fresh effort to exterminate liberty and the rights of conscience!

"Who caused the indiscriminate massacre of the myriads of innocent beings in Spain, and Italy, in the 16th century? It was the genius of papal despotism, in its bloody raide, to quench the light of the Blessed Reformation, and annihilate the claims of religious liberty!

"What moved the Spanish papists to murder fifteen millions of Indians, in South America, Mexico, and Cuba? Why, it was the devil, and the popish priests, plotting in accursed league to compel men to renounce all claims to the inalienable rights of conscience; and force upon these amiable pagans, a religion so sanguinary as to shock the most obstinate heathen!

In one word, the church of Rome has spent immense treasures, and shed, in murder, the blood of sixty-eight millions, and five hundred thousand of the human race, to establish, before the astonished and disgusted world, her fixed determination to annihilate every claim set up by the human family to liberty, and the rights of unbounded freedom of conscience!"

Echoing Baron DePonnat's thoughts, Dr. Brownlee states, "Thus the church of Rome stands before the world, 'the woman in scarlet, on the scarlet colored Beast.' A church claiming to be Christian, drenched in the blood of sixty-eight millions, and five hundred thousand human beings!"

For professing faith contrary to the teachings of the Church of Rome, history records the martyrdom of more than one hundred million people.

A million Waldenses and Albigenses [Swiss and French Protestants] perished during a crusade proclaimed by Pope Innocent III in 1208.

From the establishment of the Jesuits in 1540 to 1580, nine hundred thousand were destroyed.

One hundred and fifty thousand innocent people perished by the inquisition in thirty years.

The atrocities continue to this very day, largely ignored by Americans, who are busy with reality tv, football and baseball games, blockbuster movies and other forms of mindless, empty-calorie entertainment and distractions.

Religions Are About Control Control Control

By now, many people the world over know that modern religions are merely a control mechanism that promises much and gives little in return. Religious leaders and their employees not only do not follow the very laws they expect their followers to obey, they break many of society's laws and rules, especially moral ones.

Who hasn't heard of Catholic priests sexually molesting and physically abusing members of their congregations?

Historically, Jesuits disguised as Catholic priests systematically raped and abused nuns, church workers, and members of their flock. Their own people have, over the years, come forward with horror stories of highly ritualized and accepted rape, abuse and murder in the Catholic Church.

And when these reports and allegations come forth, what does the Catholic Church do?

Deny and lie.

In 2015, Jesuit Father Donald O'Shaughnessy, a priest for over seventy years who served in Chicago and several other places around the world, was accused of sexually abusing a man. The Society of Jesus paid out $950,000 to settle the case. The matter in question was a civil claim and as part of the settlement there is no admission of guilt or liability. According to the plaintiff's attorney, Chicago trial lawyer Eugene Hollander, the Society should have known of O'Shaughnessy's sexual predilections, as Hollander also represented another victim of Father O'Shaughnessy in a another abuse case.

How many abuse victims never came forward in his seventy years because of shame and fear?

A 2006 documentary, *Deliver Us From Evil*, recounts the tragic story of sexual abuse at the hands of a revered Catholic priest, Father Oliver O'Grady. Using interviews with O'Grady himself, confessions from numerous victims and their families, and unsettling videotaped legal dispositions of O'Grady's superiors, the movie reveals a disturbing and unforgettable portrait of sin, corruption, betrayal and innocence lost forever at the hands of the Jesuit-controlled Catholic Church.

O'Grady didn't just abuse children from one parish. When parents of the abused started asking questions, O'Grady was moved to another California mission where no one in the community, not even law enforcement, were aware of his past crimes. From 1976 to 1984 he was moved three times, from Lodi to Turlock to Stockton and finally San Andreas, until he was finally arrested as he continued to steal the innocence, break the trust, and ruin the lives of many other children.

His superiors, when subpoenaed in court, remained poker-faced and said they couldn't recall anything. They were protected at the highest ranks to sweep this pedophilia problem under the rug time and time again. O'Grady was sentenced to fourteen years in prison, but only served seven at San Quentin. After he was released, the Vatican deported him back to Ireland a free man, allowing him to walk the streets without any restrictions. Even the police weren't informed of his sexual-abuse crimes against children until an American Catholic priest, Father Tom Doyle, alerted Irish authorities in O'Grady's hometown.

After O'Grady was deported to Ireland, two of his American female victims, along with the help of Father Doyle, travelled from the US to Rome, to meet with Vatican officials. All they wanted was an apology so that they could finally find closure and begin to move on with their lives.

Not only did the Vatican refuse to see them when they arrived, they never even responded to the letter Father Doyle drafted on their behalf. According to Father Doyle, referring to the Vatican, "the institutional church not only rejected them, but re-victimized them and abused them again by making them out to be enemies of the church!"

When the documentary was released, Cardinal Roger Mahony of the Los Angeles diocese and his office were fighting sexual abuse allegations against 556 priests in the Los Angeles area alone. Mahony was responsible for moving O'Grady twice and knew of his crimes, even though he feigned ignorance in the courtroom.

Pope Benedict XVI, Mahony's superior, was accused of conspiracy to cover up sexual abuse in the US, but then-President George W. Bush, whose father George H. W. Bush was a Jesuit plant, granted him immunity from persecution. This act publicly demonstrates the immense power and influence the Jesuits maintain in America.

Father Doyle also went on to explain that "a good Catholic prayed, paid and obeyed and learned to keep their mouth shut" and "this monarchical, hierarchical system has been in place since the 4th century."

Since 1950, sexual abuse has cost the Roman Catholic Church over one billion dollars in legal settlements and expenses.

Over 100,000 victims of clergy sex abuse have come forward in the US alone. Experts say that more than 80% of sex abuse victims never report their abuse. And since 1960, 10% of the students graduating from seminary are documented as pedophiles.

Can you imagine how many more hundreds of thousands, possibly millions, of children in the US and around the world have yet to come forward out of fear, ridicule and shame?

And if they decided later in life to find the courage to come forward, many of them would be denied any financial settlements due to statutes of limitations on their claims under canon law? The deck is stacked against these abused children and their families, and the Jesuits have used this in their favor for centuries.

One can only deny and lie and cover up ill deeds for so long, before the people start to see distinct patterns of behavior that do not support the words of the Catholic Church.

To help expose US bishops who have committed crimes against children, vulnerable adults or have aided abusers, some courageous individuals have created a website, BishopAccountability.org, that reports acts of pedophilia in the Jesuit-controlled Roman Catholic Church. The website's impressive database lists all accused bishops and priests on record and is an excellent resource for learning about this dark phenomenon.

It is a matter of public record that US bishops have knowingly transferred thousands of abusive priests into unsuspecting parishes and dioceses, placing fear of scandal ahead of the welfare of children. The bishops themselves have apologized for what they call their "mistake," but this still demonstrates no accountability to victims and their families and the American people.

For true "bishop accountability," two things must happen: 1) there must be a full "account" of a bishop's responsibility for the sexual-abuse crisis, both individually and collectively, and 2) bishops who are complicit in the sexual abuse of children and vulnerable adults must, in fact, be "held accountable," i.e. prosecuted for their offenses and imprisoned.

The Jewish religion is no different, with its various scandals and instances of misconduct by leaders, rabbis and other employees of its synagogues. Jewish leaders, however, are better insulated and protected in the public eye than is the Catholic Church, because the Jesuits use Kazharjews (modern-day jews) as their accountants and bankers, and they must be well protected under law so they can carry out various geoeconomic schemes to fleece the good citizens of the world.

The Birth Of Saints

For more than 2,000 years, various Romish powers have used religion as a strict means of control over the world's population, and when the population struggled to accept Christianity, those Romish powers took pages from pagan playbooks, reinvented certain "plays" and "schemes" to fit Christian laws, and released those new rules on an unsuspecting populace.

Pagans used to worship thousands of different gods (inanimate or celestial objects), almost all of them local to a given population. There was no single "God."

To attract and convert pagans to their flock, Romish leaders invented the concept of the "saint," a previously common person (male or female, depending on which pagan crowd needed to be converted) who was immediately elevated to "sainthood" by the Roman Catholic Church. These saints then served as "gods" to the pagans, who then began worshipping them as they had their own local gods, and slowly came into the Roman Catholic fold.

In time, there evolved a saint for every occasion.

Today, we see the same pattern but, in addition to the Roman Catholic "saints," we have rock stars, sports heroes, movie megastars cartoon politicians, and comic-book superheroes.

Still, with all these clever devices, the foundation is now seeing significant cracks. Offshoot religions, which were designed to attract the strays from the traditional religions, have not worked as planned. New Age cults, serving the same purpose as the third party in politics and offshoot religions, have not gotten the large numbers of followers the Jesuits had hoped.

The New Religion: Entertainment And The Internet

The average American did not know the true power of the Internet until well after its establishment. The Jesuits did know, though, and, since it came on line, have been manipulating it to support the traditional Roman Catholic Church.

> # Like it or not, the Internet is the new religion, with its attending laws and rules and regulations, all in the form of one kind of entertainment or distraction or another.

The Jesuits have welded BigEntertainment and BigMedia with the untold power of the Internet, and have created a new more-powerful religion, the likes of which this world has never before seen. High-tech devices like smartphones and laptops and smart tvs deliver a constant stream of never-ending, mind-altering drugs that serve to draw in people of all age and stripe, and maintain them on a diet of false news and information and entertainment. And with the merging of entertainment conglomerates with communications giants, the control over America is growing ever tighter, all while good Americans are dazed or completely asleep.

Religion itself is no longer the world's keeper, and it no longer matters that it is in decline as the disseminator of Romish morals and values, because there is a more-powerful tool in use as we speak, one that caters to everyone.

The Internet—the worldwide web, email systems, SMS, and other forms of texting and message/image delivery—combined is now the most popular form of distraction on the planet, used by billions in almost every country. Cable tv, movie theaters and old-school forms are now considered dinosaurs. Live streaming and immediate downloads are expected by eager customers.

Religion certainly never had such a foothold. Even in the deepest parts of Africa, you will find cell-phone service, with the poorest folk paying out one-half of their monthly income just to have a cell phone and monthly service.

Africa: The Next Religious Frontier

However, religion is not yet completely dead, especially in Third World countries where the world's most ignorant and malleable souls reside.

In Africa, the Jesuits use the power of tv to reach millions of people with Catholic sermons and teachings each day. In the southern Africa region alone, there are more than 100 different Catholic tv programs, each with its own rabid, Jesuit-trained minister of propaganda.

Not only this, the devious Jesuits also combine each program with donation plans, whereby members can phone in—via cell phone, of course—their pledges, which are immediately debited from their meager accounts.

The Jesuits have discovered a new method of keeping the poor in their place, without employing the painstaking methods of the past: sending out missionaries to all parts of Africa, setting up schools and missions and churches to attract and convert a new flock.

Yes, the Jesuits still send out its missionaries, and today they are still building schools and churches, but the clever Jesuits are using international companies like Kentucky Fried Chicken (KFC) to help deliver the Jesuits' messages. In Swaziland and surrounding areas of South Africa, the Jesuits employ the power of fried chicken to rope in new recruits.

What's more fascinating is that they also sprout new NGOs with curious names like Kingdom For Children (also KFC). The African children quickly associate one new unknown KFC with the delicious poison sold by the other and voila! A new flock of faithful followers.

The Religion Of The Future: A New Spirituality

One might even say that today we now have hundreds if not thousands of new religions, all of which serve in one capacity or another as a means to control the American people. While not every one is completely efficacious in controlling people, they all work in concert to keep people entertained, distracted and numb to the actions and behaviors of the Jesuits. And as entertainment evolves to further influence the mind, so will new methods of controlling the population.

If we believe Jmmanuel's prophecy, then we should expect him to arrive at any moment. What then? Will there be a global reset of some kind, resulting in the cleansing of the world's ills? How will the religions of today fare? And their leaders? Will their followers be guilty by mere association and ignorance, and be allowed to study and learn the new religion?

Make no mistake, something new is coming. It may not be in the form of a religion, but it will certainly mark a reset of sorts on a worldwide scale that results in a new set of laws being handed down to us humans.

Personally, I don't see religion as a future means of control. More like a gentle philosophy of how to conduct one's life and share it with others. After all, we humans were engineered to need some form of spirituality in our lives.

We've seen that modern-day religions, which are based on the teachings of Jmmanuel, have not worked as planned, so perhaps future travelers to Mother Earth will adopt a new approach.

The alternative will be to wipe out earth's population of humans and begin anew. This also has been prophesied many times by different people of different faiths.

Whatever new method appears on our horizon, it will most likely contain similar, if not the same, teachings as before, just packaged differently and disseminated by a whole new type of religious leader. Even though Jmmanuel may not have been present the past 2,000 years, he doubtless has gotten word of our current predicament, and thus has developed a new plan.

We humans on Mother Earth are largely the same as those who were around 2,000 years ago, but with a different set of tools. We now have high-tech at our disposal, but we're still the same ignorant souls as before, with severe ignorance about our own DNA, ancient past, the knowledge and wisdom of Creation and The Universe. So we must be trained in some way, perhaps by extraterrestrials who will be patient this time, unlike Jmmanuel was during his last visit.

According to Guy Consolmagno, Jesuit astronomer and planetary scientist for the Vatican observatory and Jesuit Reverend Paul Mueller, in their book titled *Would You Baptize an Extraterrestrial?*, Consolmagno's short answer to that question is "Yes. But only if she asks!"

What are we to make of this latest Vatican stance on religion, science and outer space beings? Should extraterrestrials be feared or revered?

If we humans are to survive, we must be prepared to adopt a wholly different way of life and living, or face extinction and replacement. I feel we will be given fair warning of the next coming, and thus will be able to decide for ourselves which route we take as individuals: retraining or mass slaughter.

The choices seem simple but are far from it. The Jesuits have not prepared us at all to receive the goodness of retraining. However, we have proven as a species that we are capable of learning and adopting new methods, ways of living and conducting ourselves. Even with poor training by the Jesuits, who have steered us toward enslavement, we still can overcome our own slavery and adopt a new way of thinking, acting and treating others.

After all, it is written in our DNA, which provides us all the answers we could ever need to live a good, clean life, either on Mother Earth or off-world somewhere. It will take very special people to lead us from the current evils were we live our daily lives and step into a new unknown, one that promises a painful yet fulfilling journey to a different way of life and living.

If religion as we know it plays any part in this, the very definition must be rewritten, and also be seen by the population as a whole as something strong and positive, something to respect and admire and use as a tool for personal spiritual growth.

My personal belief is that we can start anew with a Universal kind of spirituality that offers a safe and peaceful way of living. It also should include as part of its study and practice the lost sciences, celestiophysics and astrology, both of which provide deep insights into the nature of geophysical and biophysical nature on Mother Earth.

If we adopt something entirely different, then so be it. Some of us already know and speak of its virtues. Now all we need do is convince the billions of other lost souls that share Mother Earth with us.

4

American News and Media: Keeping America Stupid

In 1671, Governor William Berkeley of Virginia wrote: "I thank God there are no free schools nor printing and I hope we shall not have, these hundred years, for learning has brought disobedience, and heresy, and sects into the world, and printing has divulged them, and libels against the best government. God keep us from both."

As the British government once told the governors of Massachusetts, "Great inconvenience may arise by the liberty of printing."

During America's prime building, from the early 1700s to the late 1800s, very few people were educated enough to read. Most could barely write their own signature.

This is what we are taught in revisionist history books and texts. How is it then that, during this nascent period in American history, there were more than 730 newspapers?

In the late 1700s alone, there were approximately 300 independent newspapers operating at the same time, servicing thousands of readers in Connecticut, District of Columbia, Georgia, Kentucky, Maine, Maryland, Massachusetts, New Hampshire, New Jersey, New York,

North Carolina, Pennsylvania, Rhode Island, South Carolina, Vermont and Virginia.

Pennsylvania and New York each hosted at least 50 newspapers. What were people interested in hearing about?

News from back home in Europe fared well. News about the American Revolution in the late 1700s and information about politics and government was also popular, because citizens were beginning to learn about the machinations of the Jesuits and how they were infiltrating foreign governments and causing much intrigue and mischief. During periods of war, citizens wished to learn what was going on and where, how their fathers and sons were doing, and what those affairs meant to their native states and regions.

How The Jesuits Designed The Newspaper System In America

Newspapers, in whatever form they came, were ink printed on paper. Most were printed by printers who were in the business to make money, primarily by printing government advertisements and announcements. Interestingly, too, all printers had to be licensed by the US government, a clear sign that the Jesuits set up the American news and media system to be limited, protected and tightly controlled.

If a printer spoke out against the government or printed something that offended someone in high standing, they could be imprisoned, lose their license, business and their livelihood. Examples of control by the Jesuit's in this system were numerous, so we will focus on just a few that had an impact.

In 1690 the first English-American news sheet debuted, *Boston's Publick Occurrences Both Foreign and Domestic*, published by Benjamin Harris. Unfortunately, his paper lasted only four days as Harris upset the English military high command by one of his comments.

In 1717, Ben Franklin's older brother James became a printer after returning from England with a printing press and paper. But just like Benjamin Harris, James ran afoul of the authorities when he offended someone in the Assembly. According to Ben Franklin, James "was taken up, censur'd, and imprisoned for a month."

During this time, Ben took over the reins of his brother's business. When the government released James from prison, it forbade him to print the *New England Courant* any longer. So Ben's name was placed on the business to circumvent the order and allow the newspaper to carry on.

In 1734, John Peter Zenger, editor of the *New-York Weekly Journal*, was arrested and charged with seditious libel for criticizing Governor William Cosby. The facts were clearly against Zenger, but a jury more sympathetic to free speech than authority acquitted him. Unfortunately, Zenger spent 10 months in jail awaiting his trial. So his wife had to take over and run the business until he was released.

Typical for any new system the Jesuits want to control, they apply their time-honored strategy of employing loyal men who dutifully follow orders. The Jesuits are a military order and, like any military, soldiers don't question a leader's orders.

The news system was no different: many hundreds of would-be journalists gathered news and information, mostly about local people and events, added advertising to cover all costs and provide a modest income for the printer, printed it on simple, four-page weekly broadsheets, and circulated the newspaper mostly to local readers who patronized advertisers and supported local politics and the economy.

This was an effective means of disseminating government (read: Jesuit) propaganda, and it served as an efficient method of controlling a population by feeding people only what the Jesuits deemed important.

In 1704, newspaperman and postmaster John Campbell served up the nation's second newspaper *The Boston News-Letter*. It lasted 72 years because he catered to the Jesuits and didn't rock the boat.

Campbell's fellow postmasters often became newspaper publishers, as well, having had ready access to information to put on their pages with the thousands of letters, government documents and newspapers from Europe. It was a treasure trove of valuable information.

Gazettes were also started by printers who had access to paper, ink and presses at hand. Ben Franklin was a postmaster and a printer and he became a wealthy publisher and editor from linking print shops and post offices in a coastal chain, and spreading newspapering up and down the Atlantic seaboard.

The Jesuits Use Media To Establish The Political System In America

A key aspect of the Jesuits' control strategy was to divide the American people, so they created the two-party political system, and they also encouraged people to pay attention to politics and governance. Before the American Revolution, the population was concerned with news about home in the Old World, and any news of loved ones in wars, battles, skirmishes abroad.

After the Revolution, people were more concerned about news about the other colonies, a Jesuit tactic that allowed them to manipulate a colony that was clearly focused on its neighbors.

Politics was forced upon the American people by the Jesuits, who made it an important part of the daily lives of everyone living in America. At least those who had access to newspapers and live information screamed from street corners and soap boxes in town.

Carol Humphrey, Oklahoma Baptist University journalism professor and secretary of the American Journalism Historians Association, said, "The primary legacy of the eighteenth century for modern journalism is the right to comment on political events. The modern-day editorial has its beginnings in that era."

Humphrey added, "Many newspapers in the 1790s were intended to accept a particular political party."

Two examples: the *Gazette of the United States for the Hamiltonian Federalists* and the *National Gazette for the Jeffersonian Republicans*.

"Their editors believed that they should support their particular party in all that they did, so they wrote essays in support of their party and included editorial comments in the news pieces that either supported their party or attacked the opposition."

This was the era when government officials and political figures—Alexander Hamilton and James Madison among them—adopted pseudonyms to anonymously promote their politics in print.

Mitchell Stephens, New York University journalism professor and the author of *A History of News*, said that the free—and free-wheeling—press of the federal period helped to create the United States: "It is hard to imagine the United States arriving when it did without a free press. It was a wild, unruly press, but democracy was a great experiment and an aggressive press was part of it."

The Jesuits directed several different wealthy and influential businessmen to buy and control newspapers, and focus their propaganda at America's working class. The wealthiest men in America directed their energies not necessarily at their own kind—financially rich, educated white people—but at those with so little.

They reasoned that this new Middle Class was in large enough numbers to crush the wealthy if they were not carefully controlled.

The Jesuits' plan worked brilliantly and was able to disseminate news and information to the American people—whatever the Jesuits felt was relevant and useful news.

And, as always, they mixed lies and deceit with the truth, making it all quite believable. In this manner, the Jesuits could teach a large population whatever it wished, and keep the population dumbed down to a level that discouraged them from asking too many questions about anything.

By the late 1880s, the Jesuit-controlled House of Rothschild had purchased or closed down almost every newspaper in the country, and began consolidating the important ones, making it easier to control the entire news industry.

They also controlled the Associated Press, United Press International and Reuters, which were the primary international news-gathering organizations that all other national and local newspapers relied on for foreign reporting and news coverage. Whenever a newspaper needed a splashy headline and were unable to cover it themselves, they simply looked at incoming wires and drew stories from them.

Effectively, the Jesuits now controlled all relevant entities of the news and newspaper industry in America, and could fabricate and release any news they wished and to the largest audience possible. This was the best means to shape a new America and her ignorant citizens, and to gently guide them in any direction.

The Jesuits Seize Control Of The New Middle Class

Newspaper magnates had already corralled America's working class, some of which would later blossom into the Middle Class. And the Jesuits had established a new method for controlling the upper crust of American society by establishing exclusive newspapers and other media for the wealthy, their families, friends and colleagues.

However, each decade brought on a new wave of discontent among the American public, and it had to be addressed. Those with the poorest education tended to be attracted to sensational stories, thus allowing them to be easily manipulated by the Jesuits. The ignorant were the most gullible and would believe just about anything, especially coming from some authority. Sadly, this has not changed today; it has grown worse.

So the Jesuits went with the flow and adopted new means of reporting news and information. In the 1920s, the era of jazz and prohibition and discontent, the Jesuits directed their newspaper magnates to issue sensational news headlines and empty-calorie stories to complement the growing nervous energy among the American people, especially her poor and ignorant and uneducated.

In the 1930s and '40s, the Great War served as a continuous distraction and also a great opportunity for the Jesuits to manipulate American minds with more clever schemes, in particular creating fear in the population. The effect was palpable: by instilling fear into hearts and minds, the Jesuits could steer the entire population in any political or social or economic direction.

When war bonds were needed, the US government sold millions at a premium. When money was needed to be raised at the national, state or local levels, taxes in one form or another would be instituted. The American people gave their last dime, if necessary. Even the poorest of the poor were coerced to donate and give and provide, all under the umbrella of American patriotism.

The Jesuits' New Propaganda Machine

A new era of propaganda was ushered in and deployed across the landscape, and it proved to be most effective, especially during times of war and conflict.

Nothing like a great war to stir up patriotic sentiment. During those times, every patriot in America, especially the loyal churchgoers, opened up his pocketbook and emptied it into the coffers of the Jesuits.

Things have not changed much today, although news and information are delivered in much slicker productions with million-dollar sets and props behind them. People have been taught to salivate over rich, colorful and loud productions, and so it was only logical that the Jesuits dolled up their news and information programming to fit the Hollywood mold.

In the 1960s, news programs were dull and lifeless, with the likes of Walter Cronkite and Harry Reasoner, two of the most insipid and mind-numbing characters ever to be featured on tv. The '70s brought in the era of the game show, and that's when we started to see a slightly different style of news program, one with a little more pizzazz.

The '80s brought forth CNN and the 24-hour news network, with more-attractive anchors and news presenters, some of whom were women. In time, these productions became more Hollywood and less real news, and evolved into the game shows we see today, replete with overly sexed-up news anchors in low-cut, spray-on tops by top designers, silicone boobs and face lifts, perfectly coiffed hair pies and dos, and gleaming million-dollar smiles.

Disneyland meets Hollywood under the twinkling stars.

Even traditionally male-dominated sports like football, baseball and hockey have news programs now that feature at least one attractive woman sportscaster among her male counterparts. These women are smart, athletic and really know the game.

Today, news is fabricated to the point of hilarity. Mass shootings are staged. Riots are Hollywood-style productions. Car crashes and scenes of war are made on the back lot of sets in some valley outside Los Angeles. Most times you can't tell the difference between a real event and one done with actors and CGI (computer generated images). We can no longer discern nonfiction from endless fiction portrayed on tv and the Internet.

So, then, how do you get accurate news today?

Fortunately, some very brave and concerned citizens have returned to the old ways: getting out on beats and talking with people, observing them and events, and then reporting on them the best they can. Blogs are now the biggest source of accurate news for discerning Americans, although the popular news sites have been hijacked by the Jesuits.

Information and comments from blogs can be a blessing or the devil in disguise. On important and controversial subjects, the Jesuits have hired misinformation and disinformation specialists that hide behind fake names and aliases. Most people never do their own research and will take the supplied information as truth and then spread it to their family and friends without any questioning.

The Jesuits also use a technique of filling up an important blog with non-comments and chatter that has little to do with the article at hand, to dissuade people from even caring about the information in article. The Jesuits' game plan is for people on the Internet to be searching for their next distraction.

Sadly for Americans, there are unlimited distractions throughout the American media.

The Jesuits Take Control Of American Media

The Jesuits have been hard at work over the last 33 years in the final push to consolidate American media. Less choice for the public means tighter control in disseminating information. The Jesuits' primary goal is to control what you think and believe and how you act.

In 1983, 90% of the American media was owned by 50 independent companies.

Today, in 2016, 90% of the American media are owned by only six companies: Comcast, News Corporation, The Walt Disney Company, Viacom, Time Warner and CBS Corporation. Direct links connect all six of these media conglomerates to the political establishment and the economic and political power-elites of the United States.

These conglomerates are in large measure responsible for shaping the social, political, economic, and moral values of adults and children in America. We're talking about 90% of what you see and hear on tv, radio, in magazines, newspapers, billboards, the Internet, etc.

If they can control a person's thoughts, they can heavily influence them in what products to buy, what foods to eat, whom to vote for, what beliefs they should adhere to, and on and on.

There's a war going on right now and it's a war for control of your mind.

Either you control what information you allow into your mind or someone or something else will.

The choice is yours.

The Media Can Legally Lie

Believe it or not, the giant media conglomerates have found a loophole in the FCC's policies that allow them to distort the truth (read: "lie to the public").

One such incident occurred in 1996 where a husband and wife investigative journalist team, Jane Akre and Steve Wilson experienced the unrelenting power of the media giant Fox.

They were developing a story about a controversial Monsanto substance, bovine growth hormone (BGH), its health risks, and its presence in the nation's milk supply. Their local affiliate station, WTVT in Tampa, Florida, was initially excited about their four-part series, but within a week, Fox executives and their attorneys wanted the reporters to use statements from Monsanto representatives, which the reporters knew were false, and to make other revisions to the story that were in direct conflict with the facts.

Fox editors then tried to force Akre and Wilson to continue to produce the distorted story. When the reporters refused and threatened to report Fox's actions to the FCC, there were both fired.

Akre and Wilson sued the Fox station WTVT and on August 18, 2000, a Florida jury unanimously decided that Akre was wrongfully fired and was awarded a $425,000 settlement. Her partner Wilson was ruled not wronged by the same actions.

Fox then appealed the case and on February 14, 2003 an appeals court unanimously overturned Akre's original settlement. The court held that Akre's threat to report the station's actions to the FCC did not deserve whistleblower protection under Florida's statute because the law states that an employer must violate an adopted "law, rule, or regulation."

In a stunningly narrow interpretation of FCC rules, the Florida Appeals court claimed that the FCC policy against falsification of the news does not rise to the level of a "law, rule, or regulation," it was simply a "policy."

Therefore it was up to the station whether it wanted to report honestly. Because of this loophole, they stated that Akre never had a legal claim against the station. The court said there was no restriction against distorting the truth.

The corporate-controlled media conglomerates can lie directly to the American citizens and pass their lies off as truth to an unsuspecting public. This is straight from the Jesuits' playbook: mixing lies with the truth and using the wholly outdated canon law, law of the high seas, and the entire US legal system to tighten their control over all American citizens.

Alternative News And Media Sources

Still, we appear to be returning to the news and information-gathering times of the 1700s, which demonstrates a clear sea change among the attitudes of the American people.

Because there are many well-intentioned journalists, researchers and whistleblowers in our communities who are fed up with BigMedia, there are quality alternative news and information resources available to Americans. Much of this information is free, while some require monthly subscriptions. Some of these resources cover a broad range of topics and others focus on specific areas of interest. The bottom line is that you have a lot of choices to acquire information and then cross-check those data with other sources to verify accuracy and legitimacy.

Many people are starting to see through the veil of the Jesuits' lies and learning about their machinations and realizing how we've been manipulated on a cosmic scale.

We no longer have to accept what we're being fed by BigMedia and BigEntertainment.

These alternative news and information resources arm us with the weapons we need to fight back and win this war on controlling our minds.

Breaking free of the Jesuit mind-control system is a revelation of thought, and lifts the human spirit to new heights of prosperity.

There is a flip-side to this goodness: the Jesuits have begun cracking down on alternative news and media websites and programming. In France, many alternative news websites have been permanently shuttered, with threats that more closings are imminent. In our own state of North Dakota, Governor Jack Dalrymple began invoking the Emergency Management Assistance Compact (EMAC), allegedly designed for states to call on other states for assistance in time of emergencies like riots and natural disasters.

That EMAC would be used for peaceful protests against oil companies in North Dakota is unprecedented, with many protestors being arrested and alternative-news journalists and filmmakers jailed on serious felony charges. Those journalists and filmmakers were simply attempting to record the events and report on them, without breaking any laws, statutes or codes.

Worse still, armored vehicles, paramilitary law-enforcement organizations and private military firms are being used against the peaceful protestors.

Just when it seems safe to get our news elsewhere, the Jesuits swoop in and destroy those safe havens.

What should good Americans do in these dangerous times?

5

American Morals And Values

"The long-feared and hated rasputitsa of eastern Europe
envelopes the morals and values of our beloved America
today, no longer confined only to one season each year."
—William Garner

We are all governed by the Laws of Creation and the
Universe, although most of us have no idea what they
actually are. Those who came before us left some clues but
nothing definitive. Jmmanuel prescribed general guidelines for living,
which he preached to his followers, but even they were often confused
about the true nature of his words and how to implement them.

Nonetheless, I extracted 124 Laws of Creation and published them
in my previous book *Arcanum*. The Laws are also posted on my website
SeanMaclarenBooks.com under the title "The Laws of Creation."

Modern religions have bastardized Jmmanuel's words and twisted
them into commandments, laws and rules, a strategy that has worked
remarkably well over 2,000 years, mostly because those forceful
teachings came at the end of a sword, whip or gun.

Pain and fear are great motivators to an unarmed population of peaceful people who wish for nothing more than being able to live a good, clean life with family and friends, and to pass on that goodness to their children.

Morals And Values Are Force-Fed To Americans

Today's system of morals and values is still preached by the Jesuits via their BigMedia, BigEntertainment, etc. and taught daily in schools, colleges and universities to millions of malleable children and young adults. Again, all highly effective. One need only look at the results: a severe decline in the moral landscape of America over the past 60 years.

Look around you to see some of these products, which include loose morals exhibited by our children, teens and young adults, at home and in public. They mimic what they see and learn in films and tv shows, trying desperately to be the next Kim Kardashian or Kanye West or Mylie Cyrus. Wearing the latest come-hither outfits that scream cheap and easy public sex and displays of raunchy sexuality. Speaking in colorful ghetto language fit for a paper king and queen.

Life imitating base art.

The Jesuits' morals and values were dictated to them by their predecessors, but they took these dictates and elevated them to a new level of depravity. For example, the Jesuits espouse adultery, assault, murder, rape, child molestation, theft, extortion, among every other type of crime on the map. They don't simply allow these acts, they insist their priests and cohorts teach all the fine points of them to followers, and beat them into everyone else.

America's Declining Moral Landscape

If you were born before the 1980s, you've directly experienced the obvious changes and been a part of the slow and methodical declination of the moral landscape in America. Those born after the '80s have also probably noticed how, as members of society, they have been and are constantly being pulled in new directions of morality (or lack of it) without any forethought. This is all by design.

The most obvious stand-out is how most of the primetime tv shows back in the 1950s through 1980s centered around the family unit and the value of family: Little House on the Prairie, The Brady Bunch, Happy Days, The Walton's, All in the Family, The Cosby Show, Good Times and The Honeymooners, to name a few. These tv shows were focused on the family unit and you never heard a curse word, rarely saw any violence or sexual-themed agendas being pushed, and the comedies were full of good, wholesome fun.

However, each of these "wholesome" shows still carried subliminal messages to the American people, not the least of which was, "Obey authority." And they were part of a much larger design to slowly introduce all aspects of morally depraved sexual situations into the American home.

Recall that the Jesuits operate on 50- and 100-year plans, allowing them to program each generation with "new" morals and standards.

Since the 1990s, the programming of the popular shows has changed dramatically from a focus on family to just the opposite: the broken family, with divorce being a viable option, single-parent households and latch-key kids.

We started to see a new kind of show, a primetime adult cartoon with mixed messages, themes and innuendos (South Park, The Simpsons, American Dad, Family Guy). There was even one infamous episode of South Park in which the goal was to see how many times the curse word "shit" or "shitty" was going to be stated.

In the end, it was hundreds. To make matters worse, South Park's four main characters are all children. This controversial episode was titled "It Hits The Fan" and aired in 2001 and again in 2005.

Replacing the family-oriented programs, the Jesuits instituted primetime tv and cable shows that focused on criminal behavior via violence, brutal deaths, prostitution, slavery, drug dealing, the prison system, etc. (American Crime, High Crimes, Sex Slaves, Forensic Files, Drugs, Inc., NCIS, Bones, Criminal Minds, Locked Up Abroad, Underworld, Inc. and all of the CSI shows), dark and twisted themes

(Revenge, How to Get Away with Murder, Scandal, Hannibal, Breaking Bad, Dexter), sexual themes and innuendo throughout (Two and a Half Men, 2 Broke Girls, Mike & Molly, Californication) and gross manipulation of others to win a prize (Survivor, The Bachelor & Bachelorette) to highlight a few.

There are also shows that not only show partial or full nudity, but promote it outright, like Dating Naked and Naked and Afraid. In Dating Naked, genitals of the contestants are blurred out, but this does little to stop the viewer's imagination. In Naked and Afraid, a man and woman, both completely naked, meet and try to survive in the wilderness together for 21 days without food, water, shelter or clothes, using only their survival skills.

Some tv shows now show graphic sex between men. Mr. Robot is only one of many shows, their intimate sex scenes built around compelling storylines that are often too good to pass up.

Parents of young children are now forced to take the time to research and subsequently block these channels from their children. This can be a challenge for a parent as there are hundreds of channels and thousands of possible programs that can be viewed and streamed from every conceivable viewing device.

Many commercials today promote outright sex-related themes including the condom, sexual lubricant and erectile dysfunction, and advertising things like rice, popcorn, ice cream, soft drinks, razors, beer, women's clothing, etc. It's thrown right in your face every day while you're watching your favorite soap opera, sporting event, sitcom, game show, news show, movie, etc. This is all by design to further erode our sense of decency and blur the lines of what we should deem as acceptable behavior.

The most obvious change in programming over the last 60 years is the rise of cursing and expletives in a variety of shows. The rules and guidelines were eased over a long period of time, but the Jesuits have succeeded in getting these once-forbidden words delivered right to your living room. As with most Jesuit programs, new themes are fed slowly to Americans over decades, making the content easy to assimilate and habituate to. After some time, Americans don't even notice the changes they were forced to endure over a long period of time. They simply take it all for granted.

Many shows now "bleep" out the expletives. The idea is to show partial censorship as a means of limiting what the viewer hears, although this actually has an opposite effect because the viewer fills in all the "bleeps" with what they think the actor actually said. The most offensive words are usually chosen in the mind of the viewer, especially if the confrontation on the screen is of a violent nature.

A long-running and successful primetime sitcom, Modern Family, heavily promotes the homosexual agenda with two married men who've adopted a Vietnamese baby girl. We now see the homosexual agenda being played out in a lot of newer primetime tv comedies, fraught with sexual innuendo and messages for the American public to consume wholesale.

For years, the Jesuits have purposefully been promoting the breakdown of the traditional family unit of a married man and woman to men marrying men, women marrying women, bisexuality and even men with multiple wives. Such behaviors have existed for thousands of years, and now they are being shoved in our faces without permission.

By allowing these types of themes to exist within primetime programming, the Jesuits are programming the public to make it acceptable and justifiable in the viewers' minds to talk and act in the same substandard manner as the actors. The main target is clearly our American youth.

And with the hundreds of cable and satellite channels and the addition of the variety of online internet streaming program choices available, we are being bombarded from every angle with a variety of endless distractions to indulge in and create new addictions for.

The term "marathon viewing" was introduced in recent years for someone who binge-watches an entire season of an online show in one sitting, practically wasting an entire day or weekend of life.

What has happened to the traditional role models of our respected parents, grandparents and teachers?

American Role Models

Today's society celebrates the horrible public behavior of so-called role models, elevating cheap acts to each evening's headline news and frontrunner entertainment.

Those who choose not to engage in it willfully remove themselves from this system that seeks to corrupt us. But the majority who remain stuck to their widescreen tv's are fed daily doses of it, parrot what they see and hear, and act out the base behaviors for the grand stage.

We see countless examples of these behaviors also being played out in public by highly paid sports figures, celebrities and politicians.

A prime example is ex-NFL football player Ray Rice who in 2014 knocked unconscious his then-fiancée in a casino elevator and then dragged her out by her hair. Nobody in public would have known about this act had it not been captured by the casino's security video cameras.

> After a very public media blitz exposing this domestic violence assault, in the end, his fiancée not only remained with him, but she chose to marry him.

Many celebrities fall victim to alcohol and substance abuse and end up in the revolving door of rehab only to relapse soon after. Politicians and high-ranking government officials project images of a squeaky-clean lifestyle, but many of them get exposed for crimes like child pornography, pedophilia, sexual misconduct, tax evasion, wire fraud, mail fraud, voter fraud, bribery, felonies, money laundering, extortion, misuse of campaign funds, perjury, obstruction of justice, destroying evidence in court cases. The list goes on.

They lose their positions or serve jail time with community service or both, and are almost immediately brought back into the Jesuit fold in another capacity, having been "rehabilitated."

These are society's role models today.

A Higher Purpose

Humans were designed and engineered to believe in a power higher than themselves. Our engineers used a form of genetic engineering, which we cannot yet fathom, to code each of our behaviors into us. They also gave us the option of free will, which few ever take advantage of. Also, The Universe itself provides its own special code that gives us our unique Map of Destiny.

This genetically programmed, built-in system is designed so we act in certain ways under various conditions. Some leeway has been granted, yes, but we normally give away this power to some external source that hijacks it for its own purpose.

The Jesuits have done just this by cleverly and effectively taking control over the human psyche through behavioral modification. The majority of Americans fall victim to it every day. Again, one only has to look around at the results to witness the accurate truth.

We are spoon-fed whatever morals and values the Jesuits wish for us at that particular time. It doesn't take much: some flashy and sexy actress or singer or dancer, or a slick politician with a smooth tongue.

One of the Jesuit's latest tactics and highly effective tools to manipulate and control the public: terms like "Trending Now," "What's Trending," "What You Should Watch."

People see these subtle commands and are immediately drawn to the names and topics others are supposedly talking and blogging about, and they absently obey the commands.

How are these lists created? An algorithm. Most of the time the names and topics that appear to be trending are actors, models, sports figures, upcoming movies, politicians, etc. The Jesuits use this tool to direct the propaganda of the day.

The names and topics in "Trending Now" change throughout the day to keep you coming back often to see what the current popular flavor of discussion is and to distract you from real issues, while simply wasting your hard-earned time. It can be the latest fashion choices, celebrity arrest, natural disaster, political viewpoint, sports team achievement or false-flag event.

The Jesuits are actually artificially creating a demand for superficial topics of discussion, and driving the behaviors of readers, viewers and listeners in some deleterious direction. Subtle and effective manipulation of your behavior.

Murder The Child In All Of Us

This is a very real phenomenon, our remaining a *child*, especially throughout adult life. Even 2,000 years ago, the Romans preached that the child must be destroyed early to make room for the adult, a loyal and subservient grown-up who would do as the Roman leadership commanded.

How could any kind and decent human being even think to kill a child? Or kill the child in all adults?

Simply put, children are the most powerful entities on Mother Earth.

They possess great power that most of us adults and grown-ups lack, because it was beaten and coaxed out of us during childhood. The child is absorbing the greatest amount of real stimuli and information from our world and The Universe. That child is capable of learning many different languages, understanding high mathematics and physics, and thinking beyond any reasonable level we adults work on each day.

The period of childhood is the most intensive time in the life of a human being, where children absorb vast amounts of information and knowledge, and act out curious behaviors to discover things by experiential experience.

The brain of a child is wired to use the maximum number of neurons during this period, to effect these important actions. The only times adults experience this "high" is during a traumatic, stressful or exciting event that produces an "adrenaline rush," or when using drugs that induce it.

I call this adrenaline rush "hot cognition," when the brain recruits thousands more neurons to perform a job that would otherwise require the normally functioning brain to use only a small number of neurons.

Only children are capable of using this complex neuronal system that's on fire 24/7 for only about 16 years. In modern American society, children are now programmed to "turn off" all sparks of their creativity and thus go numb earlier than age 16.

The Jesuits understand these complex processes all too well and so use this period in a child's life to shape and mold them into malleable and obedient little robots that will do the Jesuits' bidding at any time, especially during adulthood when they earn money that funds the Jesuits' causes. The tools of choice are BigAdvertising, BigMedia, BigEntertainment and BigPharma.

The Romans sought to kill the child so they could forge an adult who worked according to a prescribed plan, earned a meager income, paid heavy taxes, and was a slave to the Holy Roman Empire.

Today, this is exactly what we see: young children exposed to adult themes early on, designed to beat the child out of them, to create civil and docile adults and grown-ups who do as they are told and do not ask questions.

Again, how could anyone even think about killing such a beautiful entity, a gift of The Universe?

A *beautiful child*.

When people first read these words, they are outraged. Ironically, not by my revelations about this malevolent behavior by those in power, but that I would publicly bash the very power that provides the highly addictive entertainment that has so captivated American audiences for more than 100 years. How dare I attempt to educate the American people about the various means by which the Jesuits bend and twist and control our beautiful minds.

We Are All Connected

The Laws of Creation tell us that we are all connected. At this point, we all should be feeling horrible, because our children, sisters, brothers, mothers and fathers are all in great pain. How is it we cannot feel their pain? Because the very powers that feed us their messages hidden inside entertainment also include another active ingredient: a powerful novocaine for the mind, one that shuts down our gift of fear, alarm, concern and empathy.

We no longer can react in appropriate ways to warn our neighbors of the harm caused by these various insults, because we have been numbed by, and habituated to, them. In this present state, we become willing receivers of anything and everything the Jesuits feed us.

How do we break free from these bonds so we can feel once again?

Turn off the tv.

Stop watching all those hidden messages.

Stop taking those mind-numbing drugs and booze that alienate you from the rest of your connected human beings.

When you disconnect yourself from the depraved morals and values of a system that seeks to destroy your very soul, you wake up to a new dawn and begin to feel again.

You see your first sunrise.

Taste your first meal.

Smell your first rose.

Speak your first kind word.

Hear the beautiful thoughts of other human beings.

Yes, we have been programmed to believe in something higher than ourselves. I say this "higher something" is Creation itself, whatever form it comes in. We do know there are extraterrestrials among us, and they are far advanced on all levels. Imagine a being or civilization of beings that are so advanced that we cannot possibly grasp the depths of their intelligence and capabilities. Can you even imagine such a creature?

Let's say that, at this moment, we are connected to this great being, and have ready access to its soul. And let's say that this soul is the most advanced entity in The Universe. It carries all the secrets of Creation and The Universe, and those secrets are now at our fingertips.

What would we seek to know first?

What secrets are most important to us now? And how would we use them if known?

I know many people would love to design a new set of morals and values for humans. That's a beautiful sentiment.

But I offer this: why don't we simply remove the numbing chemicals from our air, water and food supplies?

Why don't we remove the toxins from our bodies and minds?

The effect?

We then will be free to feel and sense the innate good morals and values programmed into us by Creation.

And we will once again learn how to implement them for good. It's not necessary to build a whole new system of morals and values, because we already have a good and effective one inside each of us. It's just that, in these difficult times, the Jesuits have found clever ways to hide our own goodness from us.

When we break free of their thorny and toxic bonds, we will be able to experience what our ancestors lived and breathed each day, and we will then teach these morals and values to our children who will be free of external malevolence that seeks to cloud the mind and destroy the heart and soul.

We will awaken to the fact that happiness is not something we should pursue, because some piece of paper gives us the "right" to, but happiness is a by-product of being productive and doing something meaningful.

Happiness is simply a just reward from leading a clean and good life, doing what you love doing, and sharing with and teaching it to others. Happiness itself is not something to pursue for its own sake, although the Jesuits preach that we should. In fact, the Jesuits are teaching people it's good to be happy without being productive. How does this so-called happiness come about? In various forms of entertainment and mind- and body-numbing drugs.

All Americans should awaken to the fact that having good thoughts and a healthy body automatically produce the sensation of happiness. And when we express gratitude for these gifts that we ourselves actually create out of thin air, we experience even more happiness.

The Answers Are Inside Each Of Us

Each of us has all the answers inside us, but we are taught that we are ignorant fools who must obey a certain "God" and someone else's set of rules and principles.

Why follow false rules and teachings that run counter to what you "know"?

Allow your inner thoughts to replace the Jesuits' malevolent morals and values, so your goodness can surface. Spread the cheer to family and friends, colleagues and acquaintances. The more of us who wake up to our own personal power, the sooner we all will sense this collective energy.

And the sooner we harness this new-found energy, the faster we will tear down the old malevolent way of life and build a new and improved version. One that sets us on a true moral course that makes us feel good when we awaken each day, so we perform meaningful work that blossoms into a new happiness. And that happiness spreads from one person to another until it becomes an energy greater than the sum of its individual parts.

Please remember this: you are a child of The Universe, a gift to all humankind. Do not allow anyone or any entity to strip this beauty from you so they can mold you into an automaton for their own use. Keep your inner child, find meaning in your life, and share it with those you love and others around you.

King Alfred the Great, writing more than 1,000 years ago, put it well:

"In prosperity, a man forgets himself. In hardship, he is forced to reflect on himself, even though he be unwilling.

The Jesuits would have us believe their way of life for us is "prosperity." Things could not be further from the accurate truth.

6

Guns, Drugs And Sex: The Jesuits' Trillion-Dollar Worldwide Network

The biggest illegal money-makers on the planet: guns and ammo, drugs, and human trafficking, which exist wherever the Jesuits already have or wish to have political and/or social discord, leading to erosion or breakdown of a society. It has happened in every empire on the planet and it is happening now in America, although so slowly we barely take notice.

These illegal and immoral companies and groups are as organized as any successful, legitimate corporation, with Jesuit priests at the highest levels of management, and are dressed down to look streetwise and cool. They have their own brand of underground advertising, marketing and PR, some of which are directed by experts in those areas. So, while it is advertised as "illegal" across the globe, it behaves as a legitimate business that generates revenue on par with the largest businesses worldwide.

The reality is that in your home town or city, crimes like drug dealing, human sex trafficking and illegal gun sales are occurring every day without most citizens even realizing it. Just because you don't directly see these crimes being committed doesn't mean they aren't occurring. And it's not just in the low-income areas. It's everywhere. The unnerving fact is that some of your respected community leaders are involved and/or turning a blind eye toward them.

Illegal Guns And Ammo

Small arms are anything handheld for personal use: pistols, submachine pistols, carbines, rifles, and light machine guns. Light weapons include larger machine guns and grenade launchers, shoulder-fired antipersonnel and antitank rocket launchers, and mortars.

The US and China manufacture the majority of small arms used in various wars and battles today, with Chinese-made AK-47s being the most popular worldwide.

A bitter irony: the US is heavily involved in the worldwide illegal arms trade, and at home is actively attempting to disarm all of its own citizens.

The very fact that arms trafficking exists anywhere is telling: arms and ammunition are expensive, so it takes a lot of money and connections to purchase and transport illegal arms and ammo internationally. Only highly organized groups with sufficient funding can engage in arms trafficking. They are always a means to an end, so if you study the results, you may discover the reasons behind the battles and conflicts, not to mention the gunrunning in the first place.

To combat their own gunrunning and make the war on the illegal arms trade look legitimate, the Jesuits established international laws and formal groups at the United Nations. They are, of course, without teeth, but their presence conveys a certain diplomatic look that tells the world the UN is actively "doing something" to curb the sale and trafficking of illegal arms and ammunition. In reality, the UN is promoting and hiding the illegal trade of guns and ammo worldwide.

The United Nations Office for Disarmament Affairs (UNODA) reports that most conflicts today are fought with small arms. The Jesuits have designed modern-day wars, battles and conflicts in just this way to make it easy to start and stop a war. When larger weapons are used, the whole affair becomes messy and unmanageable, with too many moving parts. Small arms are easy to manufacture, sell on the black market, ship anywhere, and deliver to clients and end users.

UNODA states, "Illicit, small arms have a negative impact on security, contribute to the displacement of civilians, facilitate the violation of human rights and hamper social and economic development."

All the above consequences are precisely what the Jesuits wish to see happen in a region where they wage war. The results alone show that they succeed well, although it may take longer to reach their goals.

And when security falls in a given region, the Jesuits swoop in and emplace a new power with further restrictions on citizens' rights. Lately, the Jesuits have displaced hundreds of thousands of innocent civilians in different parts of Africa, so they can have unlimited access to new discoveries of natural resources, including diamonds and coltan. Coltan is an important mineral used in powering your iPhone and Africa has 80% of the world's supply in the Democratic Republic of the Congo.

Illegal Drugs

The US has always supplied small arms to Mexican drug cartels, fueling another big money-maker: illegal drugs. Mexico is the destination of many of the world's illegal drugs: cocaine, heroin, meth and marijuana. Some of the plants that produce them are grown in Mexico, but the majority are now cultivated in Afghanistan and Asia, far from the prying eyes of the public. From Mexico, they are moved into the US.

In America, 70% of all illegal drugs sold are supplied by the Mexican drug cartels. In recent years, Mexican Super Meth has become the drug of choice.

Heroin use doubled between 2002 and 2013 and addiction and

overdose deaths have quadrupled over the same time period. According to the CDC, an increasing number of people are primed for heroin use because they were addicted to an opioid painkiller, and heroin can be five times less expensive than opioid painkillers on the street.

In Afghanistan, the US Army has provided security for poppy fields for more than a decade, thus protecting a valuable cash crop for the production of heroin. The Russians use large Antonov cargo jets to ferry the raw product to various distribution centers around the world, where they are further processed and sent to smaller distribution centers in Mexico and the US.

How can all this manufacturing and business and transporting go unnoticed by US "authorities" and other international authorities?

At the highest levels of US Customs, DEA and BATF, people ensure that more than enough drugs enter the US market unharmed. Lower-level agents from all agencies are good, legitimate people who do their jobs well and are not involved in illegal activity. It is these people who are actually fighting the so-called War on Drugs, not knowing they are also fighting their own bosses and our US Government on orders of the Jesuits.

It boggles the mind how extensive and complex this illegal system truly is. It involves very smart and thinking people who are well educated, have extensive experience in law and business, and who are loyal to those above them. Again, most of the lower-level people are good workers who are not aware of the true nature of some of their colleagues' and bosses' illegal activities.

Trusted upper-level managers in all agencies are responsible for juggling what shipments make it to their final destinations and which ones are allowed to be confiscated and splashed all over news headlines. These Jesuit-controlled managers and supervisors must manage which of their underlings are allowed to look like the good guys who catch the criminals and who are allowed inside information to effect the goals of the Jesuits.

To say that all law-enforcement officers are crooked is inaccurate.

Most are good, loyal citizens who have families and friends who trust and admire them. And for good reason: they are trustworthy professionals.

But there also exist a group of these law-enforcement agents who are in fact criminals that answer to criminal bosses at the top. The majority of those who enter as federal agents are good, loyal people who wish to do good for all. Somewhere along the way, some of them are identified to become part of the criminal organization, and they readily accept their chosen job. It is because of criminals like these that we have this continuous War on Drugs, War on Arms, War on Terror, etc.

It makes perfect sense that good people will do a good job, and that good managers will ensure this happens all the time. And they too will have good executives who steer their progress so the company fares well in the marketplace. These companies earn millions or billions of dollars each year and provide first-rate goods and services to customers. These are the hallmarks of a good company. We see these characteristics in many local, regional, national and international firms.

Think about your favorite companies and how they function: Apple. Best Buy. Domino's Pizza. Do you see these companies posting failures every quarter or so? Do they have highly advertised losses that cause great embarrassment? Do they appear like grade-school kids doing their jobs? Are they so incompetent that they keep making the same mistakes over and over, decade after decade? Are they viewed as a bureaucratic nightmare and embarrassment?

Absolutely not.

So how is it that our own law-enforcement agencies do not follow the patterns of goodness and success we see in great American companies?

Simple: because the Jesuits control and manipulate those law-enforcement agencies to allow the illegal sales and distribution of illegal arms, drugs and humans, all for a trillion-dollar profit each year.

The drug trade is well publicized in all BigMedia newspapers, magazines and online websites. What is not publicized are the Jesuits' actions and behaviors in this vast illegal system. If people only knew and understood how the Jesuits actually functioned in these activities, they would start a riot. Or a war. And the Jesuits would not be able to control them.

How is it that the illegal drug trade is doing so well these days, with all the laws and rules and regulations in place to restrict manufacture, sale and distribution?

Do you think that it can exist on its own, that is, without the express assistance of organized US government departments and agencies?

If you just do a little research on the subject, you will soon discover that it is very expensive to have your own "organized crime network."

At an absolute minimum, you must have an extensive and complex infrastructure in place:

• Manufacturing facility or access to the product (guns, drugs or humans).

• People loyal to you and your organization, those who will not talk to family and friends about their "work activities," and who will not rat you out when they are arrested and sent to jail or prison.

• An expansive and secure distribution network that can move your product from the manufacturing facility to distribution centers in other parts of the world or the US.

• More loyal employees who will not steal from you, tell their family and friends about all the illegal guns, drugs or young women you are trafficking.

• Loyal and trustworthy people in all the law-enforcement agencies, because you and/or your employees will get arrested from time to time and will need safe passage back home.

• Loyal and trustworthy attorneys who also have "friends" at the courthouse or in the DA's office or the US Attorney's office, because you could easily go to jail or prison for decades if caught.

• Loyal fan-base of customers who regularly buy and use your product, and keep coming back for more.

• An effective advertising, marketing and PR system that gets the word out to prospective customers, users and employees.

This complex enterprise was not designed and set up on a whim.

It takes considerable time, resources, money and expertise. In this case, many decades to set up a worldwide criminal enterprise that generates many billions of dollars every year.

Only the Jesuits are capable of having this type of extensive criminal network. They have developed it over nearly 500 years, and were ceremoniously handed a series of networks from their Romish predecessors. They know exactly how to make, say, the US Drug Enforcement Administration look like a competent organization and, at the same time, have it function in favor of those involved in the illegal drug trade.

Illegal Sex Trafficking

Of the big three illegal money-makers for the Jesuits, sex trafficking of underage girls and boys is the most heinous crime of all. With guns and drugs, you have physical, inanimate objects as products to distribute to willing customers. But with sex trafficking, the "product" is an underage human who has been coerced and manipulated to become a sex slave and/or prostitute.

These underage children, some three years old, have been kidnapped or tricked and taken advantage of by someone who promised them a better life. Sex trafficking is a modern form of slavery that exists throughout the United States and the world.

Sex traffickers use violence, threats, lies, debt bondage, and other forms of coercion to compel adults and children to engage in commercial sex acts against their will. Under US federal law, any minor under the age of 18 years brought into commercial sex is a victim of sex trafficking—regardless of whether the trafficker used force, fraud, or coercion.

The situations sex trafficking victims face vary dramatically. Many victims become romantically involved with someone who then forces or manipulates them into prostitution. Others are lured in with false promises of a job, such as modeling or dancing. Some are forced into the trade by their parents or other family members. They may be involved in a trafficking situation for a few days or weeks, or may remain in the same trafficking situation for years.

Victims of sex trafficking can be US citizens, foreign nationals, women, men, children, and LGBTQ individuals. Vulnerable populations are frequently targeted by traffickers, including runaway and homeless youth, as well as victims of domestic violence, sexual assault, war, or social discrimination.

Sex trafficking occurs in a range of venues including fake massage businesses, via online ads or escort services, in residential brothels, on the street, at truck stops, or at hotels and motels. All trafficking victims share one essential experience: the forced loss of their liberty.

Commercial sexual exploitation of children (CSEC) is defined as criminal practices that demean, degrade and threaten the physical and psycho-social integrity of children. There are three primary forms of CSEC: prostitution, pornography and trafficking for sexual purposes.

For sex traffickers, the sex crimes are not about sexual pleasure, but control. They control their victims through fear, sending them mixed emotional signals, psychological torture, and if needed, threatening them with physical violence. At this point, they become a human slave.

Human sex traffickers generate hundreds of billions of dollars in profits by trapping millions of people in untenable situations around the world and here in the US. Traffickers use violence, threats, deception, debt bondage, and other manipulative tactics to force people to engage in commercial sex or to provide labor or services against their will.

The International Labor Organization (ILO) estimates that forced labor and human trafficking generates a $150 billion a year in illegal income, a very conservative estimate, considering the ILO is a UN organization that sets labor standards for all member countries within the UN umbrella. One must question how such statistics are generated.

The Jesuit-controlled UN has intimate knowledge of all these data, which it knowingly distorts to make human trafficking appear less important and less a threat to society.

Local police and volunteer organizations set up fake appointments and sting operations to attract the victims as well as catch the traffickers. Once they have a victim in a safe place, they give them the opportunity to leave and start a new life. But, for many victims, the fear of leaving their trafficker is too great. Sometimes the traffickers threaten the victim's family members as a way of keeping the victim loyal and in not trying to escape.

The anti-trafficking efforts of the police and volunteer groups are at a disadvantage from the start, because of the extensive nature of this illegal industry that is so well protected by the Jesuits.

Still, there is hope for victims and there are a growing number of groups and organizations to assist these victims to help them start a new life.

The Jesuits have in place many false-front organizations designed to look like benevolent organizations, some of which aid victims of human trafficking, making it nearly impossible to tell the good guys from the bad.

The best defense against becoming a victim within such industries is good parental care, a good sound education, and being surrounded by kind, decent and loving people.

Where can those at risk possibly find such an environment in America today?

7

The American Military: Knowing Saviors Or Unsuspecting Mercenaries?

America's military was carefully designed and built by the Jesuits, who ensured its leaders would be 100% compliant with all orders. They did this, in part, by constructing each of the military's service academies and hundreds of ROTC training units in universities and colleges throughout the US, all the while remaining behind the scenes.

ROTC, the Army Reserve Officers' Training Corps, as it exists today, began with President Wilson signing the National Defense Act of 1916. Military training had been taking place in civilian colleges and universities since 1819, but the act brought this training under a single, federally controlled entity. Army ROTC is the largest officer-producing organization with the American education system, having commissioned more than 500,000 second lieutenants since its inception.

In April 1986, the U.S. Army Cadet Command was formed and assumed responsibility for more than 400 senior ROTC units, four regional headquarters, and the Junior ROTC programs in more than

800 high schools across the country. Cadet Command transformed the ROTC from a decentralized organization, turning out a heterogeneous group of junior officers into a centralized command that produces juniors officers of high and uniform quality.

Today, Army ROTC has a total of 275 programs in universities and colleges throughout the 50 states, the District of Columbia, Puerto Rico, and Guam, with an enrollment of more than 30,000. It produces over 70 percent of the second lieutenants who join the active Army, the Army National Guard and the U.S. Army Reserve. More than 40 percent of current active-duty Army General Officers were commissioned through ROTC.

These programs ensure that the Jesuits have loyal military officers who will not hesitate to obey a direct order without thought of consequence. The ROTC program parallels the martial Jesuit Order: its loyal members are also trained to obey direct orders from their superiors. More important, they are willing to sacrifice their lives for the Jesuit cause wherever they are needed in the world.

Easily Controlled Targets

When the Jesuits planned wars, battles and internecine conflicts in the past, normally they ensured each side could be distinguished from the other by outfitting soldiers with distinct uniforms, weapons and ammunition, including tracer rounds in WWI (and later of specific colors).

Highly distinct, regulation uniforms finally appeared on the battlefield late in the US Civil War, when Jesuit military war-planners realized that war-profits would soar if they could tell exactly who all the participants were, and where and when they were engaged in battle.

Interestingly, there are few extant written complaints by officers or enlisted men of this silly tactic and strategy that clearly led to far more casualties because each side was so clearly identified. The vast majority of officers simply kept their mouths shut on the matter.

Sadly, the easiest targets of all were American Revolutionary War soldiers, most of whom who were forced to dress in prominent and gaudy costumes. The American soldier in 1781 wore uniforms with blue coats and distinctive facings for the infantry regiments from four groups of states, and the infantry coats were lined with white and had white buttons.

All troops wore white overalls and waistcoats that, again, made them stand out like . . . easy game.

To add further insult, the conventional way of meeting the enemy was via the firing line, which consisted of dozens, if not hundreds, of men in a series of lines that faced the enemy, which also was lined up in similar silly fashion. Up until that century, this method was very similar to the method of the Roman infantry, though upgraded from spears to muskets.

Thankfully, there were small units, especially of Native American origin, that defied these ridiculous orders and dressed in whatever clothing they had, providing some measure of blending in with the background setting and with the civilian population. According to the Army History Division, the period between the 1870s to 1880s saw a lack of uniformity among soldiers, due to a uniform shortage and changes to regulations that some soldiers despised.

Battles were fought according to the Jesuit method of lining up to face an enemy head on, with each side firing small arms into the line of oncoming troops. When the forward line had exhausted its single round, they took a knee so the next line could move ward and fire its single volley.

This technique resulted in a war of attrition where the winner was the side that had at least one man standing. Meantime, someone made a lot of money supplying lead and black powder (or the equivalent) to both sides.

Sounds crazy, doesn't it?

It was, but it had the desired effect. Whoever had more money and resources to produce a greater number of musket balls and other metal projectiles, swords and knives could effectively wipe out the other side.

Modern Uniform Camouflage Design

The most foolish material design was, of course, *standard* uniforms. Even with modern-day camouflage patterns, soldiers stand out like neon signs, making them easy targets. What's more, the pixelated micro and macro "digital" pattern can be distinguished electronically from any background noise because natural, organic features are generally natural and smooth, with gentle curves and swirls.

In the 1990s, camouflage developed on computers. Timothy O'Neill, "the grandfather of modern camo," pioneered the genre with his small squares of color that were able to trick the eye into seeing a camouflaged soldier or truck as part of the background of a scene. Pixels are better at mimicking fractal patterns—which our eyes interpret as white noise. By looking less like figurative "nature," digital camo gives our eyes nothing to fix on.

This gave way to a cottage industry of independent contractors and engineers hocking their own unique variant of digital camo for millions of soldiers.

Guy Cramer, CEO of Hyperstealth Biotechnology Corp, designer of camo for the armies of Jordan and Afghanistan explained that digital camouflage attempts to use advanced optical tricks to confuse the brain into missing the body of a target, rather than simply "blending in" to the surrounding landscape. He is a pioneer of algorithmic camo design, and writes programs that generate true geometric fractals.

Fractals, like the classic example of a leaf, are mathematical patterns that repeat themselves at any scale. Because they are infinitely scalable, they hide objects as small as humans and as large as buildings.

However, making that kind of visual trickery work across all environments involves ideas about color science, the anatomy of the human eye, and even the logistics of pattern-making. And it's still not perfect.

In 2004, the US Army produced a collossal failure: the $5 billion digital pattern, UCP, designed to work across all environments. The mixture of the Army's gray-green color scheme with the pixel pattern turns out to be quite eye-catching—not a good quality in camouflage.

UCP had a fatal design flaw because the scale of the patterns in the camo were badly chosen and it triggered an optical effect called "isoluminance," a phenomenon in which the eye interprets many patterns and colors as a single mass.

It made soldiers easy targets.

Deployed during the Iraq war, UCP was a failure and unnecessarily cost many American lives.

Because the US was bogged down fighting two wars, supply lines dragged and many Army soldiers had the new pixelated gray-green fatigues, but old-school gear. So "soldiers were running around with desert-colored clothing, but their backpacks, vests, and body-armor would be colored differently with black or green," essentially telling enemies where to point and shoot.

Any way you choose to examine it, the military's "digital" pattern is a screaming target, with its distinct geometric patterns that are jagged and sharp. In the future, anyone wearing this type of uniform on a battlefield will be an easy bull's-eye, given the introduction of computer-based weapons with digital optics for detection and identification.

The game is changing once again thanks to a special type of US Army night-vision goggles that detect short-wave infrared light—aka the SWIR spectrum. At $45,000 each, these goggles let soldiers see at around the 1μm-long wavelength, where colors blend together into a white mass. In other words, they make camouflage completely useless.

The problem now is that many of America's enemies have access to the same technology, thanks to a secret Jesuit network that leaks intelligence to both sides of a war, allowing any given conflict to be prolonged.

If you do even a modest study, you will discover that any "arms race" over the past 100 years was, more or less, evenly matched, because the Jesuits ensured both sides had access to similar equipment and were familiar with an enemy's tactics and strategies.

In 2014, Congress passed another NDAA, requiring a new pattern to be fully implemented across the board by 2018.

War Is Truly A Racket

Where does the money come from to fight a major war and who supplies it? For nearly 500 years, the Jesuits have funded both sides of all major wars, but very few people, even insiders, are aware of such arrangements.

Normally, it isn't until decades after any given war that the truth surfaces, although not always recorded accurately in mainstream history books. Gratefully, some diligent soldiers kept diaries that portrayed the details of each battle, and these observations were handed down in families and small communities.

In time, American towns became painfully aware that their lives were indeed controlled by a formidable force thousands of miles away in Rome, Italy. The Jesuits.

This underground history was dangerous to the Jesuits, who sent its priests and "missionaries" to these towns to rewrite history and ensure that the "correct" sequence of events and outcomes found their way into proper American history. These "missionaries" also paid or otherwise coerced residents to hand over diaries and other personal accounts, effectively suppressing the accurate history of events.

Perhaps this is one of America's greatest and saddest blunders, allowing the Jesuits to rewrite the accurate history as told by their own family members who saw events unfolding in front of their eyes.

The American forces during the Revolutionary War were often fighting Hessian mercenaries, hired by the Jesuits to fortify the British Army. Many a German soldier died on American battlefields, but they also took many an American life.

Given the Jesuits have subdued the American public with mind-numbing distractions, it no longer matters that these secrets are being reported in mainstream news media. The Jesuits have allowed this bit of history to leak out into modern history books that tackle this delicate subject, because the Jesuits know they have already subdued Americans. For the most part, though, sensitive subjects like this are almost always left on the fields of battle or in various Jesuit archives.

War still remains a great money-maker for the Jesuits, so they do not care how many American men and women are lost in battle, only that the Jesuits' goals are reached following each war.

The American Civil War: Not So Civil

During the Civil War, mercenary armies were again mounted on both sides, but this was different: both sides of the war were fought largely by Americans who thought they were fighting for the preservation of the Union or the breakaway confederate states.

To this day, traditional history books tell us the war was fought over slavery: the South wanted it in earnest but the North did not. Even though the South "lost" the war, the Jesuits got what they planned for all along: a deeply divided America with both sides hating each other for more than a century and never knowing the true reasons for such hatred.

Following the long and bloody Civil War, the US Army once again sent its soldiers on a new mission: round up the remaining Native Americans and transport the survivors to newly designated tribal lands. This had happened decades prior to the war, "relocation" of Native Americans to undesirable territories, and was begun again in earnest.

Before waves of soldiers were used in these post-Civil War operations, a small contingent of "special-operations forces" were sent in bearing clothing, blankets and other cotton- or wool-based materials, containing the small pox virus.

This germ warfare effectively wiped out thousands of Native Americans across the Midwest, creating very small colonies of Indians sitting on large patches of land.

The US government declared that, since there were so few occupants of the land, survivors had to be relocated to more suitable areas, and this is what we see today: Native Americans occupying worthless tracts of land across some of the most unusable territory in America.

Acceptance Of The Mavericks?

In time, US military units faced new wars and battles in much the same fashion. It wasn't until after WWI that a few maverick Army officers broke from rank and called for a new style of fighting, rather than face the enemy as the US military had in previous wars. General Billy Mitchell was one of these brave men who lobbied for the adoption of air power on the battlefield.

As the director of air forces during WWI, he suggested that planes be used to attack enemy ships and battlefield positions. He vehemently opposed the Jesuit's plan to build countless large battleships instead of ships capable of supporting aircraft, and was ultimately court-martialed for his being overzealous. If General Mitchell's plan had been implemented, wars would be shortened. And thus not nearly as profitable to the Jesuits.

Before Mitchell's plan could see the light, the Jesuits needed to create more formidable enemies that could engage the US military on fairly even ground and promise an extended war or conflict.

The Jesuits were in full control of the US military and designed it thereafter to be a strong force in some areas but also weak in others, a strategy that would allow the enemy to penetrate US defenses and lines and inflict heavy American casualties at prescribed times during war.

The same holds true today. We must keep something important in mind here: if the Jesuits saw that they could reach their goals without compromise, they sometimes allowed its generals and battle planners to adopt new styles of warfare. Again, provided those new plans did not interfere with the Jesuits' overall plans and goals. The Jesuits understand that some measure of "independence" among its minions is needed to keep them in line. This independence, of course, is only an illusion and extends only so far.

The Jesuits allowed some maverick generals and admirals to propose the design of aircraft carriers and new aircraft (specialized attack aircraft and bombers, equipped with heavy armament and bombs), but the Jesuits also manipulated America's enemies to adopt them, as well, so the fight was not so one sided and resulted in a quick end to a war or conflict. Again, short wars offer little or no payback.

The Jesuits carefully planned their wars and conflicts to last a certain period of time, usually years, allowing the flow of money to find its way to their coffers, and also ensuring that new land was acquired and new country lines were drawn according to plan. Other hidden agendas have been fulfilled, as well, although they still remain far from the public eye and any history book.

Today's so-called "war on terror" displays the hallmarks of Jesuit warfare: prolonged battles spread over large geographical areas, inflicting large civilian casualties that result in forced migrations of survivors.

In Europe today, immigrants are flooding into many countries and causing severe stress socially and economically, thus further dividing the European population and making it more malleable.

Birth Of American Special Operations

While there did exist "special-operations" units during the Revolutionary War, Civil War and WWI, it was not until WWII where we saw the introduction of formal special-operations units like Army Rangers, modeled after British commando units, that carried out many secret missions behind enemy lines. Most operations, though, were conducted by conventional forces.

One must wonder why this was allowed to occur, since these special units were better trained than all other units. At present, all we have to go on are the results of those battles, plus first-hand testimony from some of the men who kept accurate diaries of events. It appears that the Jesuits were planning for something "special" at the end of the war that only highly trained men could carry out.

This was, in fact, the case, as certain small units of the American Army were ordered to link up with, secure and escort out hundreds of Nazis to England and America. Conventional troops would not have been effective in these operations, although they were indeed used in support but were not given detailed information about their missions.

After President Lincoln was assassinated in 1865, the Jesuits used a special-operations soldiers from Confederate Major John S. Mosby's unit to ensure the successful escape of John Wilkes Booth.

History books now reveal that Operation Paperclip was a major operation at the end of WWII, where US special-operations troops and civilian operators under the OSS secreted Adolf Hitler and Eva Braun, and Hitler's top staff, all of whom eventually were settled in America.

The Jesuits re-wrote history to show that many of these Nazis were relocated to Argentina and other parts of South America. These reports were so effective that they launched a wave of movies, tv shows, books and articles about how Nazis fled to South America and were hunted down by diligent Nazi hunters after the war.

The Nazis Come To America

Hitler's bodyguard at the end of the war, Otto Skorzeny, was also an assassin who was used by the Office of Special Services (OSS) and later CIA on special missions. In 1943, he was brought to the US to kill beloved scientist and entrepreneur Nicola Tesla and confiscate all his papers, books, manuals and patents. Skorzeny was called upon to do several other mission inside the US, as well, then returned to Germany where he continued to fight against Soviet and American troops.

Interestingly, it was Otto Skorzeny who would ultimately betray his fellow Nazis and the CIA, many of whom did not live up to their end of a dangerous bargain. On his deathbed in 1999, Skorzeny presented a shoebox full of materials, including pictures and other damning evidence, to the boyfriend of his daughter.

The boyfriend later revealed some of the evidence in several articles and a book that exposed some of the top-ranking Nazis who had fled to the US.

George Herbert Walker Bush, Sr., alleged son of Nazi financial supporter and American traitor Prescott Bush, was one of these Nazis who was planted in the US by the Jesuits, and who would go on to lead the CIA, become Vice President, then President of the United States.

Adolf Hitler lived to the ripe age of 114 and died in the National Naval Medical Center in Bethesda, MD, in 2004. He had been living in America for decades under an assumed name.

After WWII, the US military, CIA, FBI and NASA became a safe haven for hundreds of Nazis who served the interests of the Jesuits for decades. Today, those very organizations still have the footprints of Nazi Germany written all over them.

The US military after WWII unknowingly aided in the greatest infiltration of an enemy onto American soil, and would forever be hobbled by these Jesuit actions.

Rise Of Special-Operations Units

One only need study the patterns of behavior of American forces in subsequent wars, battles and conflicts to understand this unfortunate influence. The Cold War was a carefully scripted "war" that lasted decades and cost the US and other countries millions of lives. The Soviets paid the highest price, though, losing tens of millions to the brutal regime of Stalin; like Hitler, a Jesuit priest. China also fared poorly under Communist dictatorship for decades.

If one studies the patterns of US fighting units, they will see that traditional units were used to fight most wars, but in the 1990s the Jesuits started building special-operations units on a scale never before seen in US history. As before, these special units have been used in delicate operations by the Jesuits, so we must ask what is in store for us in the near future.

Will US special-operations units be used against Americans?

During the first Gulf War in 1990, special-operations units were still relegated to small operations, most of which failed. Or, more accurately, were hobbled by the Jesuits. In Somalia in 1993, Army Delta Force troopers, Ranger and Navy SEALs were sent in to capture Somali warlords and lieutenants, but were disallowed the right equipment to effectively carry out their mission. MC-130 Spectre gunships, which had accompanied Rangers and Delta on typical training missions to "prep" the battlefield with heavy ordinance, were not allowed in Somalia.

Why? The answer remains to be seen, especially in history books, but the results suggest that American forces were not supposed to "win" these battles, only prolong them or satisfy a hidden political or economic goal. If the US military really wanted to capture Somali warlords, they could easily do so and even destroy their entire infrastructure.

Likewise, if a real terrorist wanted to kill half a battalion of special-operations soldiers on their post, base or station, they easily could. The Jesuits do not allow anything like this to happen, because it would create an imbalance in the overall war effort and possibly shorten any conflict.

In modern-day battles, special-operations forces have been called upon an unprecedented number of times, and have been heralded in the press by BigMedia and in movies and tv shows by BigEntertainment.

How is it that these very forces were not used more in previous wars and conflicts? Historians, even military, will toe the Jesuit line and tell us they were not needed or that military brass didn't know how to use them.

That's rubbish. The Jesuits have planned this for decades, and their game now is to use special-operations units because they can go into a country and carry out missions without regard for international law and in strict secrecy, except when the Jesuits want to parade these brave men around in the media. Remember: the manhunts for Osama bin Laden and Saddam Hussein and their very public accounts.

I am not bashing these courageous soldiers in any way. I served honorably as an US Army Airborne Ranger for several years and know first hand the extreme dedication of our men, many of whom are still my good friends. I also am well familiar with how the Jesuits use us as pawns in their deadly games against certain enemies, both real and manufactured.

The Lucrative War-Service Industry

Business is booming for a growing army of private military contractors who take their military training and offer it to the highest bidder. Modern-day mercenaries are stationed throughout the world, fighting conflicts for governments reluctant to use their own troops.

A private military company or private military corporation (PMC), also known as a private military security company or private force, is a non-state organization composed of professional soldiers. It provides various military services in exchange for monetary or material compensation.

PMCs are essentially armies controlled by no one but their shareholders and whoever pays them the most. They also don't have to provide details of their missions and there is very little oversight on how American tax dollars are being spent. Don't waste your time requesting a Freedom Of Information Act report because, if the government hires a contractor, the contractor doesn't necessarily have to provide any information to the public.

If the information you seek falls under any of the nine exemptions, e.g. national security information, the data will not be released. PMCs working for the US government normally fall under this exemption.

I now focus on just a few of the PMCs the Jesuits have allowed to prosper financially, companies shielded from public scrutiny: Academi (Blackwater), KBR (Halliburton), DynCorp and Raidon Tactics.

Academi is actually the infamous Blackwater, founded by former US Navy Seal Erik Prince, a right-wing Christian-supremist whose family has had deep neoconservative connections. President Bush's call for voluntary civilian military corps in 2007 granted over half a billion dollars in federal contracts to Blackwater, allowing Prince to create a private army to fight around the world.

The company's history of atrocities runs far and deep. For a while, they were even involved in a CIA "death squad."

The name "Academi," which has been in use since 2011, marks the second time the company has attempted to whitewash its name. Its first name change, to "XE Services," lasted only two years, until yet another "corporate restructuring" took place. These soldiers operate with almost no oversight or effective legal constraints and are politically expedient, as contractor deaths usually go uncounted in the official toll.

In 2007, another private military company, KBR, was awarded a multi-billion dollar contract (LOGCAP) to provide support and logistics to US troops in Iraq and Afghanistan. Like all PMCs, KBR is a highly politically connected company, a subsidiary of Halliburton that employed former Vice President Dick Cheney.

KBR used key connections to run up the costs on LOGCAP early in the wars so that future contracts would be lucrative. The third version of their contract was for $50 billion in funds, with approximately $1.5 billion in profits. Many of those dollars were unearned, as KBR grossly inflating the costs and later provided poor performance.

This indirectly affected US Army soldiers that could have had better uniforms and equipment to protect them from harm on the battlefield. In the end, the Department of Defense allowed a small cabal in the Army to give billions of American dollars to KBR. These high-ranking military officials were planning their future careers outside the military, the civilian workforce and in politics, all at our expense and the lives of our soldiers. These officials defended KBR before Congress instead of holding them accountable to the troops and American public.

DynCorp is one of the most powerful PMCs in the world, with most of its multi-billion-dollar yearly revenue coming directly from the US government. In the late 1990s, two whistleblowers (independent of each other) came forward and alleged that DynCorp employees stationed in Bosnia were routinely abusing civilians. According to their accusations, DynCorp operators engaged in sex with minors and had even sold civilians to each other as slaves. The company immediately reacted by firing both whistleblowers.

One of those who came forward, Kathryn Bolkovac, had already been facing severe difficulties before the firing. She had uncovered a network of brothels and bars where kidnapped women were forced to "entertain" peacekeepers, and her attempts to report the issue through the chain of command were ignored. Her own colleagues even threatened her life.

Bolkovac persevered. She, along with the other whistleblower, took DynCorp to court. The company lost both cases in a publicly embarrassing arena. Bolkovac's story was so compelling, it was made into a movie, *The Whistleblower*.

Raidon Tactics, Inc., a North Carolina company, enlisted veteran ex-Green Beret Special Forces operators to combat Islamic militants in Iraq, in the absence of a US military fighting force, based on a pledge by President Obama not to use US ground troops against Islamic militants. The recruits were paid between $1,250 and $1,750 per day to conduct combat missions.

The increased use of private-security personnel has raised questions, as they operate in a gray area as armed, but non-uniformed civilians.

Special-operations forces have featured prominently in Washington's military campaigns across the Middle East in what has become known as "sixth-generation warfare," defined as operations carried out by special-operations forces in conflicts that lack a clearly defined frontline, including anything from destroying core military infrastructure to assassinating political or military leaders.

Analyst Vladimir Platov says that the US doesn't deny the use of special-operations forces, but is reluctant to provide details of the operations. He goes on to state, "Washington tries its best to conceal the cases of unsuccessful missions."

The American Mercenary: Should Civilians Beware?

We are also seeing a new crop of warrior on the battlefield like never before: the mercenary, typically employed by PMCs. Even in the US, corporate military firms have been called in to police the population, and these men have acted beyond the bounds of US laws. Blackwater had a strong presence in the aftermath of Hurricane Katrina and were blamed for atrocities against innocent victims of the disaster.

As stated earlier, the Jesuits are using highly trained mercenaries to circumvent laws in America and other countries. These elite fighters can infiltrate a war zone or troubled area, perform a specific task, and leave the area without notice.

Surprisingly, the US military has also been called in on several missions inside US borders, in clear violation of the Posse Comitatus

Act, which forbids the use of US troops against Americans.

ATF and FBI agents were called in to kill David Koresh and his followers outside Waco, TX in 1993. What the American public does not know was that US Army Delta Force troopers also were present during the firebombing of the Koresh compound. When news footage was shown to a roomful of Army Rangers in the early 1990s, several Rangers yelled when they saw the faces of former Rangers who were then Delta Force operators. Not a single Ranger expressed interest in why US military troops were deployed in a firefight on American soil.

It was a telling moment in history, and frightening on many levels.

Since then, we have seen more US and foreign troops training together on US soil in preparation for uprisings and riots by US citizens. Mercenaries from PMCs also have been seen training in US cities and towns more than ever before, and never being reported in any US mainstream media, which were ordered by the Jesuits not to post any stories or images.

What BigMedia could not stop, though, was images and reports from being broadcast and printed in foreign newspapers and on websites across the globe. It appears that our foreign neighbors know more about what's going on in America than ordinary Americans do.

Also, too, several brave alternative-news websites in America have reported on these occurrences, even though their audience numbers only in the hundreds.

It is now clear that the Jesuits are planning major operations against US citizens in the coming years. They have prepared hundreds of internment camps equipped with concertina-wire fencing, body bags, and special holding facilities for US citizens.

None of this is reported in American mainstream media, though.

The US military and mercenary firms are also training alongside American law-enforcement officers. Today, it's difficult to tell the difference between a police officer and a US military soldier, as all are heavily armed with small arms, 300 rounds of ammo, body armor, Kevlar helmet and a bad attitude toward American civilians.

In the early 1990s when I went through Basic Training in the Army, several of my drill instructors repeatedly said, "I fuckin' hate civilians."

Couple that with the fact that US troops are trained to do as ordered, no matter the cost, and you have a powder keg of distrust, anger and an abject willingness to kill anyone, including innocent American civilians, and destroy our property at the drop of an order. After all, when military units have acted against civilians on American soil, the only real casualties have been American civilians. This is by Jesuit design that foments anti-war and anti-military sentiment among Americans. In short, it further divides all Americans and allows the Jesuits to manipulate us further.

One of my friends who is still in special operations, told me, after I had informed him about the Jesuits and how they operate: "I don't care. I just follow orders."

When I asked why he chose not to think for himself, he said, "I love my job. Someone tells me to go kill civilians, I do it. I don't give a shit."

If that does not chill you to the core, what will?

The Jesuits have been working special-operations warriors to the bone for many years, without upgrading their equipment to standards and sending them into battle after battle without rest. Our warriors have been fighting and dying in the longest wars in our history, in Afghanistan, Iraq, Syria and many other hotspots across the world. We now have a generation of children who know nothing other than a world constantly at war.

Is it possible that the Jesuits are intentionally grinding our specops warriors into the ground, so they cannot come to the aid of fellow Americans when the Jesuits use foreign soldiers to attack innocent American civilians?

Many possibilities abound, but the thought is compelling. After all, our own special-operations warriors are the best America produces on the battlefield. What if they were unable to come to our aid during a time of strife on American soil?

8

American Medicine
And Healthcare:
No Cure In Sight

The state of our nation's health and medical education are a reflection of our governance. As we have seen in previous areas, the Jesuits have manipulated affairs to the point of near ruin, even though Americans have yet to wake up to the fact because of continuous mind- and body-numbing programming over many decades.

Thousands of years ago, medicine was seen as a means to cure the ills of a population, while practicing good living that promoted excellent health. Students of medicine were taught state-of-the-art methods and practices that focused on prevention and cures, not merely treatments for symptoms of diseases.

The focus was not placed on specific illnesses, but a holistic or complete healthcare approach. The practices revolved around governing a person's diet and nutrition, exercise, spirituality, and relationships; every facet of a person's life. If even one aspect of a person's life was out of balance, disease and illness could occur. This process of monitoring a person's entire life with the goal of maintaining balance for overall health worked very well back then and still does today, although certainly not practiced by the American population as a whole.

Today, our healthcare and medical education systems encourage the practice of treating only the symptoms with palliative care and pharmaceuticals that keep the patient moving through a revolving door, generating billions of dollars for the entire healthcare, insurance and pharmaceutical monopoly at the expense of all Americans.

This insidious practice often forces patients into bankruptcy from extremely high hospital bills from expensive surgeries, even though most patients had some form of insurance at the time of their procedures.

We Are Taught To Ignore Our Own Bodies

Simply put, we do know how to live a good, clean life.

Some of the facts are out there. But the Jesuits have placed alongside these facts of nature a different set of laws, rules, regulations and guidelines that are advertised and marketed like high-end jewelry or a lavish lifestyle.

In short, the bad quickly usurps the good by way of a slick, sexy exterior that appeals to Americans in a way that a good, clean and healthful lifestyle never could. A hip advertisement for a McDonald's cheeseburger will attract more young people than one for bean and lentil soup, though the latter promotes better health.

Fact is, the cures for every ill in the world are available and have been for thousands of years. They are known to only a few. But these secrets are locked away in vaults and kept hidden from the general population, which is fed a steady diet of garbage in the form of irradiated pseudofoods and processed junk that contains non-food chemical additives like monosodium glutamate, aspartame, trans-fats, antibiotics, endocrine disruptors, excitotoxins and phthalates that cause a number of health issues, including cancer and diabetes.

The Jesuits' potent, long-term strategy proves that we Americans are being poisoned slowly and starved to death over an extended period of time. If the Jesuits attempted to do this over a short period, it would become too obvious and even the dumbest of the dumb would fight against it. But the Jesuits are a clever lot, taking 25, 50 and 100 years to effect their plans. Along the way, they do fail, yes, but it doesn't matter in the grand scheme because they almost always attain their goals . . . to the detriment of Americans.

The American Medical Association (AMA): Supreme Enemy Of All Americans

Where did they really begin to control and manipulate the US healthcare system? While the Jesuits have occupied America for hundreds of years, dating back to the 1600s, they have only established the foundation of America's healthcare system over the last 100 years.

In the 1800s, most people relied on homeopathy and purchased whatever remedies they required directly from a local chemist or traveling salesmen. You could keep your family healthy through affordable and readily available treatments, but mostly by good, clean living.

The Jesuits established the AMA (American Medical Association) in 1847 for the stated purpose of improving the quality of education in the field of medicine and monitoring the ethics of the practitioners. However, what the AMA quickly became in the public's eyes was a way to control competition. The AMA was the Jesuits' main tool in establishing their new form of education and healthcare in the US.

Americans were now being forced to use the Jesuits' allopathic care, a broken system that treats symptoms with pharmaceuticals, while ignoring the underlying cause of disease. By eliminating homeopathic care, the Jesuits severely curtailed Americans' freedom of choice in living a healthful lifestyle, and maintained Americans on a steady diet of poisons and unhealthful living.

The AMA controlled any form of competition by establishing universal licensing boards in all states, and establishing a commission to investigate and inspect all medical schools, including those in competition with allopathic ones.

There was nothing noble about the Jesuits' intentions, although they sold their ideas to the industry as if written on ancient stone tablets. The AMA's goal was to corral all of the physicians in the US under one umbrella organization, which meant they were all effectively controlled and could no longer practice traditional homeopathic medicine.

Hijacking America's Health

Early Jesuit missionaries and workers had already made a keen note of all the medical schools and colleges that were teaching various forms of medicine in the US. Over the years, they kept detailed records of these institutions and their practices.

In the early 1900s, the Jesuit-controlled Carnegie Foundation, a subsidiary of the Rockefeller Foundation, took those detailed records from early Jesuit missionaries and workers and compiled a complete list of all schools, colleges and universities teaching and performing any type of medical research, including those considered outside the mainstream: homeopathic, alternative, naturopathic, plus studies in pharmacognosy and related fields that emphasized using nature's own products to treat and cure the sick.

The next step in their plan: producing a special report about all of the medical educational institutions. Henry S. Pritchett, then president of the Carnegie Foundation, hired Abraham Flexner, a young researcher, author and educator whose brother Simon would later become head of the Rockefeller Foundation.

However, Abraham Flexner was not a physician, scientist, or a medical educator, although he held a Bachelor of Arts degree and operated a for-profit school in Louisville, Kentucky. Pritchett and his colleagues were concerned that a report generated by a non-physician may raise speculation.

To naive observers, Flexner was the hatchet man who would rid the US medical-education system of substandard medical schools flooding the nation. To a discerning eye, though, Flexner was the hatchet man who killed off Americans' best hope for sound medicine and healthcare.

The Jesuits chose the Carnegie Foundation to be in the vanguard of medicine and healthcare in America at that time, so Carnegie "identified improvement of healthcare in America as the primary focus of its philanthropic concern. To achieve this purpose, the foundation members correctly surmised that improvement in the very sorry state of medical schooling in America was necessary."

Curious observers would later scrutinize the Jesuits' elaborate scheme to take full control of America's healthcare and medical-education system, so the Jesuits went to great pains to cover their tracks.

> Flexner was directed to conduct an exhaustive survey that would later be twisted by the Jesuits to identify and eliminate all institutions that were teaching sound healthcare and medicine: homeopathic, alternative or naturopathic cures; those physicians who used effective remedies to cure diseases; and practitioners who showed people how to live and maintain a healthful way of life.

This approach would make way for the Jesuits' program of using synthetic drugs to treat symptoms of diseases and keep patients coming back again and again to their physicians for further treatment. The idea was never to cure a patient of a disease and resolve the underlying problem, only to alleviate symptoms with drugs produced by the pharmaceutical industry.

Flexner's report was completed in 1910, but while he was conducting his study, the AMA created the Propaganda Department, headed by Dr. Arthur Cramp, an editorial assistant at *The Journal of the American Medical Association* (*JAMA*) The committee, comprised of allopathic physicians, reviewed and analyzed various non-allopathic treatments, modalities, and services and reported their unfavorable findings to the council, which published them in *JAMA*.

This anti-competitive activity was allowed to go unchecked since its inception, though it was a clear violation of the Sherman Antitrust Act of 1890, which deemed anyone trying to monopolize trade in any way, was guilty of a felony.

Over the next 20 years, Flexner's recommendations resulted in the closing of all homeopathic, alternative and naturopathic medical schools. Its teachers and educators were "encouraged" to join the ranks of the new "allopathic" science-based medicine in the US.

The report also recommended that all "proprietary" schools be closed and that all medical schools should be connected to universities. Medical schools that offered training in various disciplines including eclectic medicine, osteopathy, chiropractic, naturopathy and homeopathy were told either to drop these courses from their curriculum or lose their accreditation and underwriting support.

A few schools resisted for a time, but eventually all complied with the report or shut their doors altogether. Those who refused were threatened, some even murdered for not participating or for revealing the true nature of the Jesuits' plan.

Most noteworthy, though, is the Hahnemann school in Philadelphia, Pennsylvania. Named after Christian Friedrich Samuel Hahnemann, considered a modern-day "inventor" of homeopathy. The school was founded in 1891 and was responsible for educating some of America's foremost medical practitioners.

Sadly, the school agreed to shift its orientation from homeopathy to allopathic medicine, demonstrating to America's homeopathic and naturopathic schools, educators and physicians that their way of life had just been shuttered in favor of the Jesuits' devious long-term plan to create a sick America. And maintain all good Americans in a state of constant sickness.

A side effect of Abraham Flexner's policy: his view that blacks were inferior. As a result, he advocated closing all but two of the historically black medical schools, Howard and Meharry. His view was that black doctors should only treat black patients and should be subservient to white physicians. Also, given his strong belief in the germ theory, argued that, if not properly treated, blacks posed a health threat to middle- and upper-class whites.

In the 1950s the AMA's policy of eliminating any and all forms of competition was well established. The Propaganda Department was renamed The Department of Investigation and as such became a clearinghouse of information and propaganda on every aspect of the alternative healthcare movement in the US. Today, the AMA website has a link to the nation's finest collection on "medical quackery, "the result of nearly seventy years of activity by the Department of Investigation.

The truth, though, is shockingly different: so-called "medical quackery" included many excellent and highly effective homeopathic, alternative and naturopathic treatments for cancer and other diseases and illnesses.

If only we had direct access to such "medical quackery" today, the Jesuits and their AMA would be out of business.

The Committee On Quackery

In 1963, to increase their control over non-allopathic healthcare choices, the AMA Board of Trustees established the Committee on Quackery to look into "targeted alternative treatments, modalities, services, products, manufacturers, and practitioners." It wasn't enough that the Jesuits had a stranglehold on the medical healthcare industry as a whole, now they wanted to further their agenda by conducting a witch hunt of all remaining non-allopathic practitioners that managed to hold on during the AMA's growing years.

The committee was headed by H. Doyl Taylor, who was coincidentally the head of the Department of Investigation. Taylor also organized a group of governmental and nongovernmental organizations that worked behind the scenes. Their sole purpose was to effectively destroy alternative medicine once and for all.

Known as the Coordinating Conference on Health Information

(CCHI) the group paralleled what the AMA's Committee on Quackery was doing except that the CCHI was a secret group, operating entirely behind the scenes and without any oversight, let alone public scrutiny.

The CCHI group's power lay in government agencies working together identifying priority targets to take action against. The Jesuits had infiltrated all of the important government agencies and would use them as they pleased to tighten their grip even further.

You will no doubt recognize most, if not all, of these agencies: American Medical Association, American Cancer Society, American Pharmaceutical Association, Council of Better Business Bureaus, National Health Council, Food and Drug Administration, Federal Trade Commission, US Postal Service, Arthritis Foundation and Office of Consumer Affairs.

These government agencies could now work together interweaving their unchecked powers to attack any and all alternative modalities. This was akin to flying a deadly night mission and dropping napalm on the entire alternative-medicine field. There was nowhere to run or hide, as the Jesuits had an unfair advantage: attacking from every angle.

Alternative healthcare was being ambushed in the worst way.

Some of CCHI's priorities also included the elimination of chiropractic, acupuncture, homeopathy, naturopathic, vitamin therapy, information on cancer treatments and other modalities, to name a few.

The CCHI and AMA served as judge and jury on what would be considered "quackery" until 1972, when William Trever brought the AMA's illegal anticompetitive activities to the public's attention with the release of his book, *In the Public Interest*. Sadly, the Jesuits suppressed his book to the point that today perhaps only one is available at any given time. The book also reveals that the AMA was targeting all "drugless healing arts," i.e. non-allopathic practitioners, especially chiropractors, more than 12,000 of whom were arrested over the years for simply practicing their art.

Over the decades, non-AMA doctors and organizations challenged the AMA's anticompetitive practices and were able to reverse some of the AMA's mandates. For example, only 30 years ago were chiropractors finally allowed access to AMA doctors' patients who requested them.

While this appears a "win" for Americans and their healthcare needs, it is a small one, as the Jesuits do occasionally allow these victories so Americans continue to have some form of hope when fighting the hidden hand that controls them.

The Jesuits' Grand Scheme

The Jesuits' goal was to reconstruct in America what they had done in Germany, where medical students were taught the "scientific method" and how to incorporate research with their studies. In Germany at that time, the Jesuits had already begun using talented German chemists to formulate the first pharmaceutical drugs that were used to "treat" patients.

Merck is considered one of the first industrial pharmaceutical firms, producing alkaloid remedies for its patients. Later, two German chemists, Charles Pfizer and his cousin Charles Erhart, would emigrate to America and start the BigPharma giant Pfizer.

The Jesuits had carefully designed and built their prototype pharmaceutical industry in the Old World, using Germany as a guinea pig, then soon exported their proven model to America, where it would serve in tandem with their newly designed medical research, medical/ science education and healthcare systems.

By the start of WWII, America's medical education and healthcare systems were in full swing, and were now poised to handle what would become their largest clients: US veterans returning home from the war.

The Cures For Diseases Are Suppressed By The Jesuits

As you can now see, the AMA does the bidding of the Jesuits, who have done an excellent job of building an organization that controls the nation's doctors with an iron fist. Almost all of the old remedies, treatments and cures for our diseases have been suppressed by the Jesuits who, through the AMA and other organizations and laws and regulations, strictly forbid any member physician to use them.

In the 1930s, there were effective cures for cancer and other ills, using different forms of electromagnetic therapy, for instance, but they and their inventors were quietly suppressed and silenced from speaking and teaching about these cures and treatments. Other inventors and practitioners of effective therapies were murdered, and their families and friends and colleagues threatened.

There still exist several classes of molecules, all plant based, that have the capacity to cure many diseases and expand human "consciousness," and the Jesuits have ensured that we never have access to them. So they make them Schedule 1 drugs that are illegal to possess, use, share or do any type of research on.

The fact that such important molecules exist at all is fascinating and worth studying. They are here with us and serve a purpose in the lives and evolution of human beings and animals that naturally ingest them.

That anyone would even attempt to restrict their possession and usage is telling: it speaks volumes about the extreme importance of these special, naturally occurring molecules and their relationship to humans.

Why would anyone attempt to deprive human beings of the ability to become a better human being?

Thankfully, some of the cures and treatments still exist today and are used by a handful of brave medical practitioners and patients, e.g. Stanislaw R. Burzynski, MD, PhD, Harvey Bigelsen, MD and Jim Humble. Their stories of success in alternative medicine have largely been suppressed to stop the spread of their discoveries.

Worse still, 50 homeopathic and holistic doctors have died over the last year, 2015-2016. The families of these men and women didn't buy the official stories from the officials about their deaths, and many have hired private investigators to reveal the truth about their sudden, mysterious deaths.

For example, the family members of deceased holistic doctor Jeffrey Bradstreet, MD hired private investigators to look into his being shot in the chest and found dead near a river being ruled a suicide. The private investigators hired for his case concluded that it was murder. Dr. Bradstreet was treating autistic children and discovered eerie parallels with vaccines given to those children. He was murdered by the Jesuits for blowing the whistle on the vaccine industry.

If only a handful of these brave homeopathic and holistic doctors had died over the past year, no one would think twice about it.

But 50?

This rises to the level of gross conspiracy.

The Jesuits aren't too concerned about it, though, as their well-established systems of medical education and healthcare are so well-entrenched that the American public is now highly skeptical of anything outside what the AMA prescribes.

BigPharma and its vaccines now advertise directly to the public with slick ads on all forms of media. How can an ignorant population ignore such "expertise"?

Together, the members of this medical and healthcare cabal control most of the planet's health concerns and needs, using synthetic drugs that do more harm than good and kill more patients than they "cure."

Our healthcare system is in shambles, yet Americans do nothing about it. People have bought into the new healthcare law's mandates, and have signed up for the relatively new illegal "insurance" tied directly to the Internal Revenue Service, another illegal corporation dressed up to look and act like a US governmental entity. Americans do so because of the Jesuits' colossal PR and propaganda machine.

It is certainly accurate that you can fool an entire nation if you have messages with high production value that are delivered again and again by "trusted" authorities or celebrities. The Jesuits dress up fiction as truth and present it to an unsuspecting public in all possible forms.

Kill The Middle Class

If you read and study the recent healthcare bill, you will see there is one group of people who pay the most in penalties for noncompliance: the Middle Class.

This is no coincidence, either. It is part of the Jesuits' grand plan to destroy the beloved American Middle Class and crush them to becoming poor, thus creating a more easily controlled two-class system.

To appreciate what I have just stated, please examine the healthcare bill and do a search for "penalty" and "penalties." Then study the outcome. It is chilling. Today, there are a dozen good documentaries and films that demonstrate the ill health of America, and some even go deep to expose some of the culprits, although no one names the ultimate human controllers of the whole mess.

I do name the true culprit: the Jesuits.

And I do so using first-rate research and studies of this organization over many difficult and challenging years. There is so much information and intelligence out there that supports all of my claims. The Jesuits no longer bother covering it up.

Why?

Because they feel they have already "won," or soon will. So why bother spending time, effort and money refuting anything said by people like me? After all, the Jesuits have Americans so well trained these days that I am considered a liar, a fraud and a "conspiracy theorist."

The Biggest Deception

John D. Rockefeller made a fortune in the oil business. His foundation gave funding to schools that taught science-based medical training and allopathic medicine. Conversely, homeopathic schools that did not use allopathic medicine did not receive any funding from the Rockefeller foundation.

To Rockefeller, allopathic medicine was a means to redistribute money he made from Standard Oil and make exponentially more money with the creation of the pharmaceutical industry, BigPharma.

Rockefeller himself preferred homeopathic medicine and had his own personal homeopathic physician treating him until he died at the age of 97. He was also a strict vegetarian. The Rockefellers, along with the Morgans and the Rothschilds, still do the bidding of the Jesuits and, to this day, serve as some of the Jesuits' public faces.

9

American Education: Church Of The Poisoned Mind

"No place can be so dangerous to the young as a Jesuit college."
—Noah Porter, Yale professor, 1851

The first schools in America were started by the earliest Indian settlers. Today they would be called informal, but the Native Americans brought together its young people in small groups and taught them basic and advanced ecology, ways of living off the land, how to live in harmony with nature, and how to appreciate and respect Mother Nature.

Sadly, history does not formally record this fact. Instead, it states that the Native Americans raped and pillaged the land, indiscriminately killed off the animals, created a wasteland wherever they settled, and made every attempt to murder the white man.

By the time the Jesuits began colonizing the New World by sending white people from the Old World, America was seen as a pristine paradise, filled with Indian savages and mosquitoes. They decided early on that one had to be eradicated, the other converted to whatever form of "religion" the Jesuits were spreading at the time. They also abolished the Native American's "informal" schooling system and quickly brought them into "proper" schools, or disregarded them altogether.

Regardless of what recorded mainstream history tells us, the fact is, the Jesuits were responsible for designing and building America's first schools and school system. They continually fought against the Puritans, whom they eventually infiltrated and controlled, and thus created new institutions that, in the least, were in the shadow image of the Jesuits.

If you study the history of education across the planet, you'll see that people like Native Americans were interested in harmonic life with their surroundings. Their history tells us that they were visited by different species of extraterrestrial beings who gave them intimate knowledge about the Universe and Mother Earth and all life. Much of this information was suppressed by the Jesuits, who rewrote that part of history in an entirely different light.

Most historical schools taught their young some form of Christianity as the basis of their education system. The earliest formal colleges were all religion based and produced all the religious leaders and workers of the day. The leaders in those times, 500 years ago and back, were chosen from royal bloodlines and given formal teaching by religious scholars who secretly controlled and manipulated them.

The New American University: Controlling The Minds Of The Elite

The first colleges and universities in America were all in the northeast: Harvard, William and Mary, University of Pennsylvania, etc. All were modeled after the multidisciplinary system of Oxford and Cambridge Universities in England, both of which were designed and built by Romish powers based on their own Italian educational system, in particular the University of Bologna, regarded as the first formal education institution in the world.

Of course, the Chinese may argue the point, as they had formal schools long before the Italians and English, but history ignores this.

In America, the Jesuits sought to attract the best and brightest students, to form their young minds in the ways of Jesuitism, so they could become the leaders in all areas of government, law, politics, medicine, etc. Today, it is not much different: those regarded as the "best" schools in the nation are located in the northeast and still produce the vast majority of leaders in all fields.

Among the current elite Jesuit Catholic Ivy League universities you'll find Georgetown, Notre Dame, Boston College, Holy Cross, Villanova and Holy Cross at the top of the list. The Jesuits have built the ultimate education system in less than 500 years.

From *Catholic Higher Education in America: The Jesuits and Harvard in the Age of the University* by Kathleen A. Mahoney:

"As the largest and most influential group of Catholic educators, the Jesuits have functioned as a bellwether for much of Catholic higher education; thus their responses to the academic revolution reveal a great deal about the broader state of American Catholic higher education.

"Founded in 1540 by Ignatius of Loyola, the Jesuits garnered immense fame over the centuries for their remarkable exploits in the remotest corners of the globe as explorers, missionaries, pastors, political operatives, and educators. In the field of education their achievements were unparalleled.

"By 1773 their educational institutions numbered eight hundred, forming a vast network of schools—one that, according to historian John W. O'Malley, the 'world had never seen before nor has it seen since.'

"In 1900, Jesuit institutions of advanced education could be found in Europe, the Middle East, the Far East, and throughout the United States, where the Jesuits' ventures in higher education began in 1789 with the establishment of Georgetown Academy, which evolved into the nation's first Catholic college.

"With colleges subsequently established on the East and West coasts, in the Pacific Northwest, Midwest, and the deep South, the Jesuits came to dominate Catholic higher education in the nineteenth and early twentieth centuries, with approximately two dozen colleges under their direction by 1900. Currently there are approximately 230 Catholic colleges and universities in the United States; twenty-eight, including some of the larger and more notable, are sponsored by the Jesuits. No other religious order has come close to this number.

"Revered by their supporters and reviled by their foes, the Jesuits brought to their legendary labors in education two critical, complementary resources that go far in explaining their striking success. The first was the *Ratio Atque Institutio Studiorum Societatis Iesu*. A plan of studies formalized in 1599 after decades of trial-and-error experimentation, the influential and widely emulated *Ratio Studiorum* set forth the aims, principles, methods, and pedagogical strategies that came to define Jesuit education.

"The second resource the Jesuits brought to their work in education was less tangible but no less important: in the section devoted to education, the Constitutions of the Society directed Jesuits to adapt their educational practices as necessary to suit the "places, times, and persons" they encountered. The balance struck between the structure of the *Ratio Studiorum* and the flexibility encouraged by the Constitutions served the peripatetic Jesuits immensely well, whether in the courts of China, the jungles of Latin America, or frontier outposts along the Mississippi.

"In the middle of the nineteenth century, Yale professor Noah Porter (1811–92) heard the reverberations of the Reformation and Counter Reformation echoing across America's academic landscape. In 1851, Porter penned a ninety-five-page tract, *The Educational Systems of the Puritans and Jesuits Compared*, as part of an evangelical Protestant effort to garner support for college-building efforts in America's West.

"For Porter, who served as Yale's president from 1871 to 1886, the Puritan epitomized the quintessential American Protestant; the Jesuit embodied the essence of the despicable 'romish church.'

"Using the two as archetypes for the Protestant and Catholic in education, Porter distilled the history of higher education in the United States into a long academic battle for the nation's soul, in which the Puritan principles of education as practiced in Protestant colleges produced the most agreeable political, social, and religious ends, while Jesuit colleges imperiled the commonwealth religiously and politically.

"According to Porter, Jesuit colleges on American soil threatened the very future of the United States as a Protestant nation."

> It is abundantly clear that our nation has been designed and built by the Jesuits, who also have created an impressive system of education for our young. They mold and prepare our young students for further studies and future work in America's Jesuit Matrix, which promises them the American Dream and a seat at the head table.

Even if most of these students do not make the grade and become a member of the "elite," they still serve dutifully as the Jesuits' soldiers.

The Jesuits train the world's PhDs and MBAs, primarily at American universities, and they go forth and land jobs at the highest levels in all areas and in all countries. America is also famous for training the world's dictators, despots and martinets at our various military academies and postgraduate schools.

Shackled To Debt

Colleges and private schools cover their financial aid offices with posters and pamphlets depicting smiling, happy students with hopes that these student loans will allow them to complete their schooling and follow their lifelong dreams. What they don't realize is that it's really just predatory Jesuit banking propaganda drawing them in, using the latest deceptive marketing ploys. Most students have no idea they'll end up with credit card-like interest rates, not a low-interest, small payment as they had been led to believe.

Note that there are differences between the federal student loans and private, bank-backed student loans. Unlike federally backed student loans, which give borrowers the option of income-based repayment plans or deferring payments altogether in cases of financial hardship, private lenders, like Sallie Mae loans, are under no such obligation and have no incentives to offer any repayment flexibility.

And after a student graduates with their expensive degree and can't find a job to make ends meet, many graduates are forced to choose bankruptcy to get out from under the crushing debt. Bankruptcy is no longer an option to discharge student debt, thanks to the government's 2005 "reforms."

You can now only discharge student debt in cases of extreme hardship, such as total and permanent disability.

However, disabled people are still responsible for paying taxes on any money used to repay student loans. In most cases, this tax burden is well over $10,000. How can a disabled and now-unemployed person possibly pay such a debt, living on a modest fixed income from total disability? The Jesuits have lured in many good Americans, who then discharge their debts, only to be hit with a large income tax bill at the end of the year. All along, some of these good people, in particular veterans with 100% disability, would have been better off simply by not repaying the student loans, as the IRS cannot garnish the bank accounts of veterans, for example, to pay a tax debt.

The American student loan system is designed to shackle aspiring students with debt before they even graduate and find a job, that is, if they actually graduate at all. The Jesuits have young students right where they want them: already in debt to the banks before they are able to establish a career.

Assuming the graduate gets a job and starts paying back what seems like an insurmountable loan sum over a number of years, they can then look forward to taking on even more debt in purchasing a car, a house and other symbols of success that the banks will somehow allow for if they can just "make the payment" over many years, even decades.

The Jesuits have designed the credit system to keep people in debt their entire lives. In their system, students are treated like criminals if they can't find a way to pay back their debts, a system that, unbeknownst to them, entrapped them from the start and took advantage of their unbridled enthusiasm for the promise of a good education and the American Dream.

The Choice Charade: No Child Will Escape

The Jesuits have designed the American public school system, community colleges and universities, using federal aid as a means to control and manipulate young Americans.

Charlotte Thomson Iserbyt, former Senior Policy Advisor in the US Department of Education, blew the whistle in the 1980s on government activities withheld from the public.

In her book, *The Deliberate Dumbing Down of America*, she talks about "the choice charade" and how the public continues to be misled as the local school districts continue to lose their hold of control over time.

"A careful warning was sounded through National Defense Education Act Amendment of 1961—Additional Views when the Congressmen said, "We reject that there can exist Federal aid to any degree without Federal control. We further hold that there should not be Federal aid without Federal control.

"The public has been misled to believe that "choice" in education means more parental freedom to determine the best educational placement for their children. This is not what 'choice' means to education reformers. 'Choice' to these reformers is a tool—a tool to advance education reform from point A to point Z.

"The public school system in America has maintained, until now, a representative form of government. Localities would elect a school board which had legal oversight over the curriculum, staff, budget, programming and planning of the community's school, being directly accountable to parents, taxpayers, voters and citizens. Each new phase of education reform in the past three decades has adversely impacted this original system of accountability and oversight. But the worst is yet to come.

"Parents traditionally have had the right to educate their children at a public, private, religious, parochial or home school. But this is not what the reformers mean by 'choice.' Their 'choice' is a Trojan Horse entering society under the guise of vouchers, tuition tax credits, charter schools and their many hybrids.

"Reformers' 'choice' is not free choice. Reformers' choice always places additional governmental structures between parent and child, voter and representative, citizen and state. The reformers' 'choice' will only reveal its true nature in the end, when it becomes manifest as a rigid, intrusive, and controlling plan for children, families and society.

"These reformers are change agents who intend to use 'choice' to maneuver reform towards their pre-determined goals. This purposeful deception has been wildly successful. So successful, in fact, that some reformers have noted that they are well ahead of schedule in implementing their planned transformation. In a few short years this 'choice' will be fully operational.

"All families with school-age children (public, private and home) will feel the brunt of this deception. Recall the title of the bi-partisan Washington education mega-bill, No Child Left Behind. No child will escape. Every child will be affected."

Now just substitute the word "reformers" with "Jesuits" in the above paragraphs and read it again. The Jesuits' intentions will be revealed in plain sight. Their goal is always to divide people, pit one group against another then conquer both sides.

They've successively been doing this throughout the centuries and continue to this day. It's their modus operandi, their calling card. And it is wildly effective.

The Ordinary American Student

Our educational system today is so dumbed down that we as a

country rank near the bottom of every list of excellence. This is not a coincidence, either.

When choosing a group of people to act as "immigrants" and instigators of riots and uprisings in a country, the Jesuits always select the most ignorant, those with little or no formal education who are also deeply passionate (read: very aggressive and quick to riot).

There are more universities and colleges and community colleges than ever before, each over-charging students in tuition and fees that follow students for many years, if not decades. Yet the quality of education is so much lower.

There is only one explanation: it is all by clever design.

The Jesuits learned early on that they could control an ignorant population more easily than an informed and armed one.

The Jesuits developed the education system that produced the Enlightenment, which was the incubator of the secular humanism that drives organized learning in modern America. For all the good that Jesuit educational norms may have done, their bottom line, sad to say, is a national dumbing-down.

You can see this reflected in a survey by the National Association of Scholars (NAS) of *US News & World Report*'s annual listing of "America's Best Colleges," private and public. NAS found that in 1914, 90% of the elite colleges required the study of history. In 1939 and 1964 that figure had shrunk to 50%. By 1996, only one of the 50 best schools offered a required history course. Even the elite schools weren't spared.

Voltarine de Cleyre, in her 1932 writing, *Anarchism & American Traditions*, gives her view on the importance of teaching history:

"It was the intention of the Revolutionists to establish a system of common education, which should make the teaching of history one of its principal branches; not with the intent of burdening the memories of our youth with the dates of battles or the speeches of generals, nor to make the Boston Tea Party Indians the one sacrosanct mob in all history, to be revered but never on any account to be imitated, but with the intent that every American should know to what conditions the masses of people had been brought by the operation of certain institutions, by what means they had wrung out their liberties, and how those liberties had again and again been filched from them by the use of governmental force, fraud, and privilege.

"Not to breed security, laudation, complacent indolence, passive acquiescence in the acts of a government protected by the label 'homemade,' but to beget a wakeful jealousy, a never-ending watchfulness of rulers, a determination to squelch every attempt of those entrusted with power to encroach upon the sphere of individual action—this was the prime motive of the revolutionists in endeavoring to provide for common education."

Prior to the advent of today's modern computer technologies, physical books were the tool of choice to educate the masses. With more and more of today's courses now being offered online, the Jesuits have a new tool to manipulate and change history at will. The Internet's worldwide web is fast becoming the repository of false history, misinformation and disinformation.

The Jesuits do this to muddy the waters and confuse the already ignorant population, to put multiple versions of history out on the Internet. This is all by design to create many different versions of events so that the real truth can be hidden. But who would be the wiser? Who would even notice with a little history change here, a little there, over time?

Historical information residing in physical books was much harder to change or manipulate because you could look up established history, passed down through multiple generations. But once historical information is put online, it can be easily modified and manipulated by the stroke of a few keys with rarely anyone noticing except for maybe a few. Those who are in control of a school curriculum for history studies in digital book content have the ability to easily modify history.

History can be written and re-written to fit whatever agenda the Jesuits want to pursue. Most people are so distracted these days with their smart phones, endless apps, and meaningless instant messages that they fail to see the gross manipulation of our own history taking place behind the scenes. These same children absorb and not question any of it.

Why would they?

They do what they're told in school, or else.

Sadly, most people won't even put up a fight when it comes to history and will accept whatever version they're told because they don't want to spend hours upon hours doing quality research to reveal what the true history was for a particular topic. For them, it's just too much work to confirm a piece of information about a historical event. They'd rather watch Duck Dynasty, Pawn Stars, The Real Housewives of [Wherever], or review the latest Facebook posts.

After all, why should one need to know anything about their country's own history and its leaders?

In America, most of our students have been deprived of a great education. It's not because they are dumb. I have had the pleasure of working with hundreds of America's young, and found them to be smart and thinking, eager to absorb and learn new disciplines and practices, and dying to make significant contributions in their lives and the lives of others.

These are good students who are the products of a sinister system that seeks to maintain them at the lowest economic and scholastic levels possible. Only the bright and obedient rise up the Jesuit ranks to stardom where they are further manipulated to do as ordered, their loyalty rewarded with a lavish lifestyle and a little power.

Most of our children, however, cannot even calculate the correct tax on a store purchase, give the correct change at a fast food drive-thru, have a vocabulary sufficient to converse with customers at Walmart. Their only desire is to get off work as soon as possible and "hang" with friends and chat on the latest cool app.

The youth today are firmly entrenched in the Jesuit Matrix, as their daily habits are dictated by Jesuit programming from public schooling, tv shows, movies, blogging, online social media, the worship of professional athletes, celebrities and self, etc.

We good Americans have not produced these children.

The Jesuits have.

And they've poisoned their beautiful minds in the process.

But Americans are complicit in the Jesuits' scheme to disarm our children of their ability to think for themselves. Instead, the Jesuits have created a world of automatons who do as they're told, act according to what pop culture says, buy what BigMedia tells them to.

Today, we have a nation of young slugs who do not question authority. And if they do, they do not act any further. Questioning is not enough. One must study, learn, then act in the interest of all.

When these kids wish to "learn" something new, they "Google" it or visit Wikipedia for answers.

I Google information all the time, even though most of what I seek is not available on the upper reaches of the worldwide web. But I find Wikipedia to be suspect on all levels and an endless land of drivel.

Before the Internet age and search engines like Google that returned an answer to a question in mere seconds, people were limited to physical print media like books, encyclopedias, professional magazines and actual experience to acquire information about a particular subject or topic. In most cases, the only place to find such information was a local library.

Even 10 years ago, libraries were essential to researching valuable information. It took a lot of time and effort to do research, and people were much more careful with how they spent their time. They valued their time and their acquired information like a prized possession, having no computers, scanners or digital cameras to instantly save their researched information to.

They had prized book collections and hand-written or typed documents placed in binders, usually with no backup system. All their information was gotten from physical libraries.

Closing our public libraries is yet another agenda of the Jesuits. If they control all of the information digitally, we have to accept what they present to us in limited choices. The less choice we have, the easier it is for them to manipulate us into following their preset agendas while they modify historical data to suit their purposes.

With the Internet today, you have information effortlessly at your fingertips and the ability to converse with someone in a different physical location almost instantly.

So this is what we've come to—
Google and Wikipedia? Seriously?

But this is a double-edged sword: most people never take the time to look at multiple sources online and offline to corroborate its validity and integrity. They simply take whatever is presented to them as absolute fact and, these days, even fighting to defend their new-found information.

How many of us ever question the fast and free information presented to us in milliseconds?

How many of us take the time to check the original source of an article, the news we are being presented from BigMedia or information searches from Google or online "libraries" like Wikipedia?

We're all being led astray by the Jesuits in many different ways and we don't even realize it. We must take back from them the responsibility of controlling our thoughts. And we cannot expect a quick fix in our society of instant gratification. Collectively, we have the power within each of us to do it, but it will take a concerted effort, a lot of patience and making incremental positive changes over time to remove the poisons from our minds so carefully emplaced by the Jesuits.

10

American Criminal Justice: Protect And Encourage The Criminal

The complex legal and criminal justice system in America is in shambles. It sometimes functions well for small civil issues and in matters of trade, and it appears to work against crimes and their criminals in some areas ... some of the time. But can you find any consistency in how laws are followed, how crimes and criminals are dealt with from one city or region to another?

If you follow trends over the last 50 years alone, you will easily see several distinct and disturbing patterns:

- The criminal justice system favors the criminal
- Judges hand down lenient sentences to criminals for violent crimes
- Violent crimes are not being punished to the extent as many white-collar crimes
- The criminal justice system encourages crime and criminal behavior on an unprecedented scale, which has led to increased false-flag attacks on civilians and law-enforcement officers

The Jesuits are encouraging more and more first-time criminals to engage in more criminal behavior that extends to violent crimes.

Witness the meteoric rise of police brutality caught on videos that suddenly go viral, leading to more and more violence from both sides, law enforcement and the public.

The overall effect is to create fear and anxiety in the population, which is an effective way to get Americans to demand stricter laws that "protect" them.

Though you may not realize it, this "protection" leads to subjugation of Americans' Constitutional rights.

A Rigged System

The Jesuits designed the criminal justice system to appear as a fair and balanced system that deals adequately with crimes and those who commit them. But when you look underneath the surface, you soon find that the system is rigged against certain parties (ethnic, economic, geographic, etc.), and favors certain criminal behaviors. Sometimes the effects are subtle, so a population cannot realize the true intent, but lately it appears that the Jesuits do not care if their machinations are discovered and revealed to the public.

That thought alone is frightening, because it suggests that their end game is near. . . .

Old-World Justice Is No Longer

Small, close-knit, hierarchical, religious communities marked the colonial period. The courts were a secular arm of the church. Colonial criminal justice systems reaffirmed the community's religious aim and reflected popular culture.

America's criminal justice system was imported from the Old World, which believed in ceremonial punishments in full public view. This method deterred crime quite effectively, unless the powers that be in that town, city or country wished to usher in new stricter laws and rules. In those cases, crimes were artificially designed and carried out to effect specific goals.

Depending on the crime committed, punishment in colonial America could be very harsh and long lasting. Because the laws were directly tied to some version of the Bible and what was deemed as sinning, citizens had to be mindful, as people were always watching others in such small communities.

On the subject of sex, the Bible only approved of "straight" sex. Acts like masturbation, fornication, adultery, sodomy and buggery (bestiality) were all punishable offences. Whipping, branding and public shaming were common. For offenses like slandering, nagging and gossiping, a device called the brank was used. It was a heavy iron cage that fit over the offenders head and had an iron plate that rested on the tongue, sometimes with spikes.

Other penalties: branding letters onto the hands, cheeks or foreheads, nails hammered into a criminal's ears and nose, depending on the severity of the crime. There were also whipping posts, unique devices like the ducking stool and pillory, which caused great pain public shaming at the same time.

The public perceived criminals as members of the community that had gone astray, so the courtroom was an opportunity for them to repent. Reintegrating them into the community was the common goal; incarceration was rare, but not absent.

However, if a criminal was sentenced to prison, he was subjected to medieval exercises like the treadmill. Inmates were forced to continuously step on revolving steps on a giant revolving barrel. Sometimes the barrel turned another mechanism that ground grain or corn. Other times it was simply a torture apparatus.

Inmates also turned other forms of manual milling machines. The most popular was inside a circular room that had a large wheel in the center and several long heavy wooden arms extending outward for inmates to pull or push. The effect also ground grain or corn, but as with the treadmill, they sometimes did it for "exercise" and daily punishment.

But as vicious as colonial punishments were, there was a relatively simple way to avoid the worst of them, the gallows, by pleading "benefit of clergy." This loophole dated from the Middle Ages and applied to anyone who could read a certain passage from the Bible. The original tilt was in favor of priests and monks, since most laymen could not read. A lot of men, women, and even slaves, who didn't know how to read, figured out how to memorize the verse and were able to escape hanging. Magistrates eventually caught on to this trick.

James A. Cox elaborates:

"Every Virginia minister was required to read the *Articles, Lawes and Orders* to his congregation every Sunday, and, among other things, parishioners were reminded that failure to attend church twice each day was punishable in the first instance by the loss of a day's food. A second offense was punishable by a whipping and a third by six months of rowing in the colony's galleys. Which underlines the notion of the law as an arm of religious orthodoxy."

Imagine if this were true today.

We no longer see such "encouragement" from any religion or church, because religion in general is no longer seen as the best means of controlling the population, which now is handled via various forms of entertainment and the Internet. Today, the public believes that church and state are largely separated, although behind the scenes the Jesuits and their followers still carry on using demonic practices.

Today's Laws Shape Society's Behaviors

Civil, commercial and criminal laws are in place to force and shape the population to adopt certain behaviors or to discourage them. So it is informative if you examine some of these laws and rules then study the subsequent collective behaviors of our society and the events that transpired during and after the same period.

In general, the Jesuits were very clever to enact civil and commercial laws that staunchly promoted trade and boosted the nascent economy in America. They built the infrastructure of America and created new laws to protect their interests.

All this occurred over more than 200 years. It took this long to build a stable economy, capable of sustaining itself locally, regionally and nationally, and also through well-established international trade, especially in the highly lucrative slave trade.

Once America reached a certain point of prosperity, in the late 1800s, the Jesuits changed the laws from promoting the economy to *regulating* it.

If something is going so well and generating thousands of jobs and income for many people, and creating great success stories, why would you then want to regulate and control/manipulate it? The answer is simple: the Jesuits then had 100% control over America's economy and its laws, and could manipulate both whenever they wished or when celestiophysics favored their doing so.

Exporting American Laws

Although America's laws and regulations were taken directly from England's (and, of course, Roman law), the laws in our country quickly evolved into a different system entirely, one that would shape the entire world.

American slavery and racial laws lasted for more than 200 years, with racial laws today being largely hidden from society but still present. The legal and criminal justice systems were designed to protect the slave owner and land owner. Slaves themselves had few if any rights, only spare privileges at the whim of owners.

This system of laws and regulations very quickly produced a two-class system: owners and slaves.

The slaves lived in fear and anxiety, which over time gave rise to discontentment and resentment. Those in turn evolved into curiosity and anger. Curiosity gave way to education, anger to hatred. In the end, the system produced an educated slave who distrusted, feared and hated the white man, and all he had and stood for.

The Jesuits satisfactorily built a new system in America that soon saw the emergence of new criminal enterprises that featured former slaves and their descendants. When the Jesuits forced immigration, America's African Americans soon had new minority neighbors, with whom they fought for territories and rights.

Hunting The American Family

The evolution of the legal and criminal justice systems later moved on to the American family unit, which the Jesuits desperately wished to control and manipulate. In the 20th century, laws and rules were drawn first to protect the family as a whole, then to protect the child and mother. Women's rights did not exist previously, but soon came into effect. The rights of children were also nonexistent but they too came into being.

The Jesuits forced Americans not only to recognize but also respect these new rights of the previously disenfranchised. On the outside, this appears benevolent, but in effect it allowed the Jesuits great access to women and children, which they brought into the national spotlight even further by putting mothers to work and encouraging them to "fight" for equal rights. Children were ordered into schools that effectively took them away from their parents and gave the Jesuits much time to mold and shape them.

Recall what former Yale President Noah Porter said about the Jesuits:
"No place can be so dangerous to the young as a Jesuit college."

In time, the Jesuits created yet another two-class system: the husband and wife, both fighting against each other for "rights." Children too got in the act by demanding more and more from parents. Add to this family stew, "Child Protective Services," often accused of unfairly removing children from non-offending, non-violent mothers, causing further discord within the family unit. The resulting discord has resulted in sky-high juvenile crime in the largest cities, with the criminal justice system being overloaded and overwhelmed on all levels.

The Welfare State: Obedient And Subservient

How clever that the Jesuits first build up a system to prosperity, then control and manipulate it to the point of destruction and decay. This is what we see today in our society, clear examples of systems that once thrived, and were later torn to shreds. What we see today is a fragile shell of our former, once-prosperous country, the New World.

The criminal justice system does work to some degree, because the Jesuits always allow some success stories. They advertise those effectively to the citizens of America as "proof" the system, while not perfect, works well and protects Americans.

Unfortunately, those successes are few and far between and do not accurately reflect the what occurs in America's society today. Americans fail to see the true nature of our collective problems, because they are too wrapped up in working to earn enough money to cover massive debts, getting lost in endless forms of entertainment, caring for too many children, doing drugs, committing crimes. We are blinded to the very acidic behaviors and actions that are eroding our society down to threads.

The Jesuits have created an efficient welfare state in America, a large obedient population that does not question authority, but simply collects a check each month for basic necessities. Why do so many of our children resort to criminal behavior and crime?

The Jesuits encourage these behaviors because it further erodes our society and creates a larger rift between the haves and have-nots. The Jesuits facilitate and encourage this behavior through violence in popular music, tv programming, movies and sensationalized high-drama news stories.

Take, for example, a popular primetime tv show, Dateline, that plays multiple episodes per month. Every new story seems to be about a mysterious murder, rape, kidnapping or missing person's crime happening in small-town America. Dateline serves up heavy doses of fear.

Yes, these crimes do happen, but Dateline wants us to feel as if every small town in America is experiencing these heinous crimes every single day.

The Jesuits, in an indirect way, propagate and justify these horrific, deceptive and grotesque crimes, depicting them as normal living conditions in small-town America, conditions we then are encouraged to accept and not question.

We must see programs like this for what they really are: mind-control programming that prepare the audience to accept what they see on tv and in movies as the norm and what is to come in the near future. In effect, this cancerous system numbs and habituates Americans to the painful reality of crimes and criminals, thus allowing both to perpetuate virtually unnoticed. And when they are noticed by Americans, they are readily accepted.

Incarceration Nation

An average of 168 per 100,000 people are incarcerated in the whole world. Today, in the US alone, 743 per 100,000 people are in prison.

Russia is a distant second.

We have approximately 2.2 million of our US citizens behind bars in a country of roughly 320 million. The US Department of Justice estimates that 5.1% of the US population will serve time at some point in their lifetime. That's one in every twenty citizens ending up in prison.

Between 1880 and 1980, the rate only grew from 125 to 200 per 100,000, a modest increase over a 100-year period with population increases. But from 1980 to 2010 the rate grew from 200 to 743 in only 30 years. What has driven this rapid rate over the last several decades?

Again, it is by design: to further erode American family bonds, instill fear in all of us, and to accept whatever conditions the Jesuits hand us.

For-Profit Prisons

Beginning in the early 1980s, the Jesuit's established a new source of income: the "for-profit" private prison system. They were already making money in the illegal drug, gun and sex-trafficking businesses, so why not make money off of incarcerated prisoners?

It's a win-win, no lose situation for the Jesuits: they make money when their drug dealers are selling drugs and when they wind up in one of their prisons.

The three biggest US private prison companies, Corrections Corporation of America (CCA), GEO Group (formerly Wackenhut Corrections Corporation) and Management & Training Corp. (MTC), were all established in the early 1980s, at the same time the prison population started to increase rapidly.

The Sentencing Reform Act of 1984 created the US Sentencing Commission, responsible for sentencing guidelines for the US federal courts.

State and Federal prisons, in an attempt to save money and taxpayer dollars at a time when states were confronted with enormous fiscal crises, were directed by the Jesuits to outsource the responsibility of incarceration to private prisons and create an entirely new industry. The idea sold to the public was that a private company would run more efficiently than a state or federally run entity and would save money, thereby helping the state balance sheets and saving the taxpayers money over the long term.

However, this was just another Jesuit ploy. The private prison companies locked the states into contracts strict with occupancy requirements: 80-100% capacity. Now the states were beholden to the private prison companies and could be fined if the prisons weren't filled to near-capacity, based on what their contracts explicitly stated. Whether crime was on the rise or decline, these private prison corporations made a lot of money.

In addition to having an incentive to keep the prisons at full capacity with state compliance, companies like CCA and the GEO Group also involved themselves in helping to write the "three-strike" and "truth-in-sentencing" laws to ensure that prison populations continued to rise.

The top three private prison corporations noted earlier gave $45 million over the last 10 years to political parties, to influence policies. CCA has also employed hundreds of lobbyists, and until recently had a seat on the American Legislative Exchange Council, which drafts model laws. The CCA lobbies for longer sentences and making laws easier to break, so that they have a steady influx of new prisoners coming in which is great for business.

Needless to say, business is booming.

According to the ACLU, companies like CCA and GEO Group perform a public function, get most of their revenues from the government, and yet are relatively free from public accountability. They are exempted from complying with Freedom and Information Act requests.

CCA and other private prison companies are shielded from public scrutiny by a veil of secrecy, despite locking up nearly 130,000 prisoners and an additional 15,000 immigration detainees each year, while receiving billions in government dollars.

Today, for-profit companies are responsible for approximately 6% of state prisoners, 16% of federal prisoners and, according to one report, nearly half of all immigrants detained by the federal government.

Last year, in 2015, CCA had revenues of $1.726 billion, and GEO Group approximately $1.66 billion. CCA's profits have increased more than 500% over the last 20 years. CCA boasted a profit of $2,135 per prisoner and GEO Group outdid them at $3,356 per prisoner last year.

These are not corporate numbers we should admire and be proud of. The private prison system has grown into a $70 billion business.

Modern-Day Slavery

Up until the mid-1960s, two-thirds of the US prison population was white. Today, it is overwhelmingly black, all by Jesuit design.

In the US prison system, a prisoner aged 50 and older costs about $68,270 a year to house. Whereas, younger prisoners of color (African American and Latino) average only $34,135 annually. In NYC last year, the average cost to house, feed and guard each inmate was $168,000.

In the private prison system, the contracts allow the corporations to "cherry pick" whatever prisoners they want to house. Economically, it makes economic sense to choose younger prisoners because they cost about half the amount of older prisoners.

The for-profit private prisons not only have to turn a profit, but they have to please their shareholders as well. The goal of a private prison is to make money, so the traditional state or federal prison mandates of rehabilitation take a back seat in a private prison. Also, private prisons want to retain custody of their prisoners longer and keep the prisons at full capacity, so they have no incentive to rehab a prisoner for early dismissal. Private prisons also cut costs with healthcare and accommodations, and there is more violence within the private prison system, most of which goes unnoticed and unreported to the American public.

The private prisons rely on young African American and Latino prisoners for their very survival as a business.

Another disturbing trend in the private prison system: patients with mental health issues that have been forced from state hospitals into prisons where they don't get anywhere near the medical and psychiatric help that they need. They are more likely to get beaten up and raped in the private prison system, without any oversight or protection from within.

Getting Rich Off Prisoners

Imagine owning a company where all of your employees showed up every day for work, were reliable, hard workers and didn't collect any benefits or pensions. This would be the ideal workforce, wouldn't it? It's exactly what the private prison system has designed, using their outrageously affordable labor pool.

State, federal and private prisons all have a dedicated workforce of cheap labor at their disposal. State and federal inmates make on average between 23 and 97 cents per hour worked. Great for the private prisons, and bad for many industries in the US.

With the threat of losing migrant workers because of new immigration laws, some of the private prisons have contracted with farms to replace migrant workers with prisoners. The prison system has found a way to bring business back to the US from foreign countries like China, with this huge pool of cheap, endless labor.

It's no longer farming and producing license plates: protective military gear, law enforcement equipment, McDonald's uniforms, furniture, Honda car parts, dentures, jeans sold by Kmart and JCPenney, prisoner call centers, processed beef and other meat products, and Victoria Secret lingerie being sewn by female prisoners in South Carolina.

One such company, Unicor, once known as Federal Prison Industries, manufactures 175 different products from 109 prison factories, supplying an array of goods to the DOD, DOJ, USPS, and others.

Hundreds of iconic American companies are exploiting prisoners to sell you products. Investment companies like Fidelity, a funder of ALEC, is deeply invested in supporting CCA and the GEO Group. Chances are, if you have a 401(k) with Fidelity, some of your money is being invested in the private prison industry.

Fidelity is just one example of hundreds of American companies that work with private prisons for financial gain.

Beyond just private prisons, there are other companies reaping huge profits from the Jesuit-created police state: the bail industry, property seizure by local and state police, prison healthcare through Corizon, phone-service providers for prisoners through Tel-Link, and others that take advantage of prisoners and their families by fleecing them of whatever money they have left or have to beg for or borrow.

A glaring example: non-offenders can have their personal property taken away in certain states, if the police "suspect" their involvement in a crime committed by someone else. One elderly couple lost their house because their adult son sold $40 worth of marijuana from their front porch without their knowledge.

Former Vice President Dick Cheney and former Attorney General Alberto Gonzales were indicted in a South Texas county and brought up on charges for illegal detention practices in federal prisons. Cheney was indicted for investing in Vanguard Group, which holds financial interests in private prison companies that run holding pens for illegal immigrants in South Texas. Gonzales was indicted because he allegedly used his position while in office to stop a 2006 investigation into abuses at one of these privately run prisons. Unfortunately, neither will not face any jail time.

What does the future hold for private prisons that reply on keeping prisoners within their walls for as long as possible? The recidivism rate in the US is about 60%, which means that private prisons can expect just over half of the inmates who get out of prison to return again, keeping private prisons profitable and on a path of continued growth.

Regarding a study done on the private prison system, David Shapiro, former staff attorney at the ACLU National Prison Project states, "The study is an example of the many ways in which for-profit prisons create an illusion of fiscal responsibility even though the actual evidence of cost savings, when apples are compared to apples, is doubtful at best. Privatization gimmicks are a distraction from the serious business of addressing our addiction to mass incarceration."

Where does this leave us? Private prisons have been marketed as the necessary supplement to save taxpayer dollars. It is a system designed by the rich and for the rich and clearly relies on the incarceration of African American and Latino citizens for its continued survival.

The future of crime fighting in America and all over the world will get even more complicated when the international police organization INTERPOL accepts as its leader a Chinese law-enforcement official, Meng Hongwei, China's vice minister for public security and a former head of Interpol China.

With China's systematic abuse of its own innocent citizens, how should America view this appointment?

The Jesuits are further preparing America for despotic rule under a dark Asian cloud. I discuss the "Chinafication of America" in a separate chapter in an upcoming book in this series, *Romanic Depression*.

References

"If we encounter a man of rare intellect, we should ask him what books he reads."

—Ralph Waldo Emerson

[Author unknown] (1768). *The Jesuit Detected; or the Church of Rome Discovered in the Disguise of a Protestant, Under the Character of An Answer to All That is Material in the Rev. Mr. Hervey's Eleven Letters to the Rev. John Wesley.* J. Johnson, London.

[Author unknown] (1859). *The Constitutions of the Free-Masons.* Robert Macoy, New York.

Multiple authors (1839). *The Principles of the Jesuits: Developed in a collection of extracts from their own authors, to which are prefixed a brief account of the origin of the order and a sketch of its institute.* JG and F Rivington, London.

Multiple Authors (1902). *Concerning Jesuits*. Catholic Truth Society. London.

Achilli G Reverend (1851). *Dealings With the Inquisition; or, Papal Rome, Her Priests, and Her Jesuits. With Important Disclosures*. Harper and Brothers Publishers, New York.

Astle D (1975). *The Babylonian Woe: A Study of the Origin of Certain Banking Practices, and Their Effect on the Events of Ancient History, Written in the Light of the Present Day*. Published as a private edition. Toronto.

Balla I (1913). *The Romance of the Rothschilds*. Eveleigh Nash, London.

Barrow I (1852). *A Treatise of the Pope's Supremacy: To Which is Added A Discourse Concerning the Unity of the Church*. Johnstone and Hunter, Edinburgh.

Baxter R (1835). *Jesuit Juggling: Forty Popish Frauds Detected and Disclosed*. Craighead and Allen, New York.

Bellows HW (1871). *Church and State in America*. Philip and Solomons, Washington, DC.

Bert P (1880). *The Doctrine of the Jesuits*. BF Bradbury, Boston.

Berk MA (1842). *The History of the Jews from the Babylonian Captivity to the Present Time*. MA Berk, Boston.

Bigelsen H MD (2009). Medical Conspiracy in America. Menagerie Design and Publishing, Nevada City, NV.

Black AN (2015). Here are 6 Companies That Get Rich off Prisoners. http://www.attn.com/stories/941/who-profits-from-prisoners. Accessed and vetted 06 November 2016.

Bolton HW (1890). *Patriotism*. Meyer and Brother, Chicago.

Breig J (2003). Colonial Williamsburg That The Futre May Learn From The Past: Early American Newspapering. http://www.history.org/Foundation/journal/spring03/journalism.cfm. Accessed and vetted 06 November 2016.

Bright K (2016). Modern Day Slavery: For Profit Prisons Make Huge Profits But Degrade Us All says Whistlebloser Kiriakao. http://www.opensourcetruth.com/2016/03/04/modern-day-slavery-for-profit-prisons-make-huge-profits-but-degrade-us-all-says-whistlebloser-kiriakao/. Accessed and vetted 06 November 2016.

Brownlee WC Reverend (1857). *The Secret Instructions of the Jesuits*. American and Foreign Christian Union, New York.

Brzezinski Z (1983). *Power and Principle: Memoirs of the National Security Advisor, 1977-1981*. Farrar, Straus, Giroux, New York.

Brzezinski Z (1997). *The Grand Chessboard: American Primacy and Its Geostrategic Imperatives*. Basic Books, New York.

Brzezinski Z and Scowcroft B (2008). *America and the World: Conversations on the Future of American Foreign Policy*. Basic Books, New York.

Bungener LF (1855). *History of the Council of Trent*. Harper and Brothers, Publishers, New York.

Burke-Gaffney MW SJ (1944). *Kepler and the Jesuits*. The Bruce Publishing Company, Milwaukee.

Burnet G (1816). *The History of the Reformation of the Church of England, Volume I, Part II*. Clarendon Press, Oxford.

Butler SD (1935). *War is a Racket*. Round Table Press, New York.

Campbell WJ SJ (1921). *The Jesuits, 1534-1921: A History of the Society of Jesus from Its Foundation to the Present Time*. The Encyclopedia Press, New York.

Carlson JR (1943). *Under Cover: My Four Years in the Nazi Underworld of America: The Amazing Revelation of How Axis Agents and Our Enemies Within Are Now Plotting to Destroy the United States*. E.P. Dutton and Company, New York.

Cartwright WC, MP (1876). *The Jesuits: Their Constitution and Teaching. An Historical Sketch*. John Murray, London.

Casten L (2010). Project Censored The News That Didn't Make The News: 11. The Media Can Legally Lie. http://projectcensored. org/11-the-media-can-legally-lie/. Accessed and vetted 06 November 2016.

Caulkins, C (2015). Society of Jesus Settles Another Sexual Abuse Claim involving Father Donald O'Shaughnessy. http:// legalbroadcastnetwork.com/the-lbn-blog/2015/7/3/society-of-jesus-settles-another-sexual-abuse-claim-involving-father-donald-oshaughnessy. Accessed and vetted 06 November 2016.

Chiniquy C (1886). *Fifty Years in the Church of Rome*. Fleming H. Revell Co., New York.

Chiniquy C (1900). *Forty Years in the Church of Christ*. Fleming H. Revell Co., New York.

Clements J (1865). *History of the Society of Jesus From Its Foundations to the Present Time*, Volume II. John P. Walsh, Cincinnati.

Coape HC (1910). *In a Jesuit Net: A Story of France in the Time of Louis XIV*. The Religious Tract Society, London.

Cooke R Dr. (1985). *The Vatican Jesuit Global Conspiracy*. Manahath Press, Hollidaysburg, PA.

Coorlim L and Ford D (2015). CNN: Sex Trafficking: The New American Slavery. http://www.cnn.com/2015/07/20/us/sex-trafficking/. Accessed and vetted 06 November 2016.

Coppens C SJ (1911). *Who Are the Jesuits?* B Herder, St. Louis.

Corti EC Count (1928). *The Rise of the House of Rothschild: 1770-1830*. Cosmopolitan Book Corporation, New York.

Corti EC Count (1928). *The Reign of the House of Rothschild: 1830-1871*. Cosmopolitan Book Corporation, New York.

Coudrette C (1761). *Mémoires pour servir à l'histoire générale des Jésuits, ou Extraits de l'histoire universelle de M. de Thou*. Octavo, Paris.

Courson BFMN (1879). *The Jesuits: Their Foundation and History, Volumes I and II*. Benziger Brothers, New York.

Cox JA (2003). Bilboes, Brands, and Branks: Colonial Crimes and Punishments. http://www.history.org/Foundation/journal/spring03/branks.cfm. Accessed and vetted 06 November 2016.

Coxe AC Bishop (1894). *The Jesuit Party in American Politics: Exposed and Expounded in Letters to the Ablegate*. American Citizen Company, Boston.

Creighton C (1996). *Operation James Bond: The Last Great Secret of the Second World War*. Simon and Schuster, London.

Crowley JJ Reverend (1912). *Romanism: A Menace to the Nation*. Jeremiah J. Crowley, Cincinnati.

Crozier AO (1912). *U.S. Money vs. Corporation Currency: "Aldrich Plan." Wall Street Confessions!* The Magnet Company, Cincinnati.

Cusack MF (1891). *What Rome Teaches Us*. The Baker and Taylor Company, New York.

Cusack MF (1896). *The Black Pope: A History of the Jesuits*. Marshall, Russell and Company, London.

Daniel TC (1911). *Daniel On Real Money*. The Monetary Educational Bureau, Washington, DC.

Daniel TC (1912). *High Cost of Living, Cause-Remedy*. The Monetary Educational Bureau, Washington, DC.

Daniel TC (1916). *The Betrayal of the People*. The Monetary Educational Bureau, Washington, DC.

Daniel TC (1917). *The Real Issue, Democracy Against Plutocracy*. The Monetary Educational Bureau, Washington, DC.

Daniel TC (1919). *No Plutocratic Peace But a Democratic Victory*. The Monetary Educational Bureau, Washington, DC.

Daniel TC (1924). *Real Money Versus False Money—Bank Credits.* The Monetary Educational Bureau, Washington, DC.

De Cleyre V (1932). *Anarchism & American Traditions.* The International Anarchist Publishing Committee of America: Free Society Group, Chicago, IL.

De Saint-Priest A Count (1845). *History of the Fall of the Jesuits in the 18th Century.* William Clowes and Sons, London.

Desanctis L with Betts M, Translator (1905). *Popery, Puseyism, Jesuitism.* [Original title: *Roma Papale.*] D Catt, London.

Dewey ER and Dakin EF (1947). *Cycles: The Science of Prediction.* Henry Holt and Company, New York.

Dowling J Reverend (1845). *The History of Romanism: From the Earliest Corruptions of Christianity to the Present Time.* Edward Walker, London.

DPE Research Department (2014). The U.S. Health Care System: An International Perspective (Fact Sheet). http://dpeaflcio.org/programs-publications/issue-fact-sheets/the-u-s-health-care-system-an-international-perspective/. Accessed and vetted 06 November 2016.

DPE Research Department (2016). University of New Hampshire Health Services: Traditional Chinese Medicine. http://dpeaflcio.org/programs-publications/issue-fact-sheets/the-u-s-health-care-system-an-international-perspective/. Accessed and vetted 06 November 2016.

Duff A (1852). *The Jesuits: Their Origin and Order, Morality and Practices, Suppression and Restoration.* Johnstone and Hunter, Edinburgh.

Duffy TP, MD (2011). Yale Journal of Biology and Medicine: The Flexner Report – 100 Years Later. http://www.ncbi.nlm.nih.gov/pmc/articles/PMC3178858/. Accessed and vetted 06 November 2016.

Du Jarric P SJ (1926). *Akbar and the Jesuits: An Account of the Jesuit Missions to the Court of Akbar.* Harper and Brothers, New York.

Dye JS (1864). *The Adder's Den: or the Secrets of the Great Conspiracy to Overthrow the Liberty of America.* John Smith Dye. New York.

Eckel LSJ Mrs. (1874). *Maria Monk's Daughter: An Autobiography.* The United States Publishing Company, New York.

Eksteins M (1975). *Limits of Reason: The German Democratic Press and the Collapse of Weimar Democracy.* Oxford University Press, London.

Elon A (1996). *Founder: A Portrait of the First Rothschild and His Time.* Viking, New York.

Evans TR (1888). *The Council of Trent: A Study of Romish Tactics.* The Religious Tract Society, London.

Farrell JP (2010). *Babylon's Banksters: The Alchemy of Deep Physics, High Finance and Ancient Religion.* Feral House, Port Townsend, WA.

Fergusson A (1975). *When Money Dies: The Nightmare of the Weimar Collapse.* William Kimber, Ltd. London.

Feval P (1880). *Jesuits!* (Sadlier AL, Translator) John Murphy and Company, Baltimore.

Foundation for Rational Economics and Education (2003). An address to the US House of Representatives by the Hon. Ron Paul of Texas entitled, Sorry, Mr. Franklin, "We're All Democrats Now." January 29, 2003. Foundation for Rational Economics and Education, Lake Jackson, TX.

Fulton JD (1856). *The Outlook of Freedom: or The Roman Catholic Element in American History*. Moore, Wilstach, Keys and Overend, Cincinnati.

Fulton JD (1888). *Washington in the Lap of Rome*. W. Kellaway, Boston.

Fulton JD (1889). *The Fight With Rome*. Pratt Brothers, Marlboro, MA.

Fulton JD (1889). *Rome in America*. The Pauline Propaganda, Boston.

Gade RW Major (1994). The University of Dayton School of Law: Crime and Punishment in American History (book review). http://academic.udayton.edu/legaled/crimlaw/. Accessed and vetted 06 November 2016.

Gerard J SJ (1897). *What Was the Gunpowder Plot? The Original Story Tested by Original Evidence*. Osgood, McIlvaine and Company, London.

Gibson D (2015). The Washington Post: 5 Lessons from the Resignation of Bishop Robert Finn (Analysis). https://www.washingtonpost.com/national/religion/5-lessons-from-the-resignation-of-bishop-robert-finn-analysis/2015/04/21/d1317f48-e843-11e4-8581-633c536add4b_story.html. Accessed and vetted 06 November 2016.

Gilens M and Page BI (2014). Testing Theories of American Politics: Elites, Interest Groups, and Average Citizens. American Political Science Association. *Perspectives on Politics*, September 2014/Vol. 12/No. 3.

Gilmore IV (1914). T*he Federal Reserve Act of 1913: History and Digest.* The National Bank News, Philadelphia.

Griesinger T (1885). *The Jesuits: A Complete History of Their Open and Secret Proceedings from the Foundation of the Order to the Present Time, Volumes I and II* (Scott AJ, Translator). WH Allen, London.

Grinfield EW (1853). *The Jesuits: An Historical Sketch.* Seeleys, London.

Haeckel E (1910). *The Answer of Ernst Haeckel to the Falsehoods of the Jesuits.* The Truth Seeker Company, New York.

Hansen JO (2015). The CNN Freedom Project: Jada Pinkett Smith's fight to end US trafficking, Children for Sale: The Fight to End Human Trafficking. http://www.cnn.com/videos/intl_tv-shows/2015/07/28/freedom-project-children-for-sale.cnn. Accessed and vetted 06 November 2016.

Hoensbroech PV Count (1911). *Fourteen Years A Jesuit: A Record of Personal Experience and a Criticism.* Cassell and Company, London.

Hughes T (1910). *History of the Society of Jesus in North America, Colonial and Federal.* The Burrows Brothers Company, Cleveland.

Ives JM (1936). *The Ark and the Dove: The Beginning of Civil and Religious Liberties in America.* Longmans, Green and Company, New York.

Jackson L (2015). Sputnik News: Top Secret Ops: Washington Relies Heavily on Special Forces in Middle East. http://sputniknews. com/middleeast/20151228/1032398264/us-special-forces-seals.html. Accessed and vetted 06 November 2016.

Jefferson T (1903). *The Writings of Thomas Jefferson, 20 volumes, Volume 10.* Published by the order of the Joint Committee of Congress, issued under the auspices of the Thomas Jefferson Memorial Association. Andrew A. Lipscomb, Editor-in-Chief, and Albert Ellery Bergh, Managing Editor. Washington, DC.

Joly M (1864). *Dialogue in Hell Between Machiavelli and Montesquieu.* A. Mertens and Son, Brussels.

Kauffman LS (1922). *Romanism as a World Power.* The American Publishing Company, Philadelphia.

Kearns K (2015) http://www.breitbart.com/big-government/2015/11/05/full-tpp-text-reveals-a-very-bad-deal-for-america/. Accessed and vetted 06 November 2016.

Kidder DP (1851). *The Jesuits: A Historical Sketch.* Lane and Scott, for the Sunday-School Union of the Methodist Episcopal, New York.

Kinser A (1966). *The Works of Jacques-Auguste de Thou.* Martinus Nijhoff, The Hague.

Kroll A (2013). This Is How Private Prison Companies Make Millions Even When Crime Rates Fall. http://www.motherjones.com/mojo/2013/09/private-prisons-occupancy-quota-cca-crime. Accessed and vetted 06 November 2016.

Lash JL (2006). *Not In His Image: Gnostic Vision, Sacred Ecology, and the Future of Belief.* Chelsea Green Publishing, White River Junction, VT.

Lathbury T Reverend (1838). *The State of Popery and Jesuitism in England; from the Reformation to the Period of the Roman Catholic Relief Bill in 1829: and the Charge of Novelty, Heresy, and Schism Against the Church of Rome Substantiated.* John Leslie, London.

Laurens JW (1855). *The Crisis or, The Enemies of America Unmasked.* GD Miller, Philadelphia.

Laynez D (1824). *Secreta Monita Societis Jesu: The Secret Instructions of the Jesuits. With An Appendix.* LB Seeley and Sons, London.

Lease M (12 August 1896), Cooper Union Hall, New York, NY. www.spartacus.schoolnet.co.uk/USApopulistP.htm. Accessed 12 April 2010, 08 December 2011 [as of 30 April 2015, no longer available; please see www.gilderlehrman.org/history-by-era/populism-and-agrarian-discontent/essays/mary-elizabeth-lease-populist-reformer for biographic sketch; Accessed and vetted 30 April 2015.]

Lehmann LH (1944). *Behind the Dictators: A Factual Analysis of the Relationship of Nazi-Fascism and Roman Catholicism. Second enlarged edition.* Agora Publishing Company, New York.

Leone AM (1848). *The Jesuit Conspiracy: The Secret Plan of the Order.* Chapman and Hall, London.

Lester CE (1845). *The Jesuits*. Gates and Stedman, New York.

Lindbergh, CA (1913). *Banking and Currency and the Money Trust*. National Capital Press, Inc., Washington, DC.

Livingston J (1986). *Origins of the Federal Reserve System: Money, Class and Corporate Capitalism, 1890–1913*. Cornell University Press, Ithaca.

Lord J (1886). *Beacon Lights of History*. James Clarke and Company, New York.

Luke JT (1851). *The Female Jesuit; or, The Spy in the Family*. MW Dodd, New York.

Luke S Mrs. (1852). *The Sequel to The Female Jesuit; containing her previous history and recent discovery*. Partridge and Oakey, London.

Lutz A (2012). Business Insider: These 6 Corporations Control 90% of the Media in America. http://www.businessinsider.com/these-6-corporations-control-90-of-the-media-in-america-2012-6. Accessed and vetted 06 November 2016.

McCabe J (1913). *A Candid History of the Jesuits*. GP Putnam and Sons, New York.

McCabe J (1916). *The Tyranny of Shams*. Dodd, Mead and Company, New York.

McCabe J (1939). *The Papacy in Politics Today, 2nd Edition*. Watts and Company, London.

McCarthy MJF (1904). *Rome in Ireland*. Hodder and Stoughton, London.

McCarty B (1922). *The Suppressed Truth About the Assassination of Abraham Lincoln.* Self-published by Burke McCarty, Washington, DC.

Macarow A (2015). Our Prison System Is Even More Racist Than You Think. http://www.attn.com/stories/2419/racism-in-american-criminal-justice-system. Accessed and vetted 06 November 2016.

Macaulay TB (1849). *The History of England From the Ascension of James the Second.* Bernard Tauchnitz, Leipzig.

Maclagan E Sir (1932). *The Jesuits and the Great Mogul.* Burns Oates and Washbourne, Ltd., Publishers to the Holy See, London.

Macpherson HC (1914). *The Jesuits in History.* Macniven and Wallace, Edinburgh.

Magevney E SJ (1899). *The Jesuits as Educators.* The Cathedral Library Association, New York.

Makow H (2009). *Illuminati: The Cult That Hijacked the World.* Silas Green. Winnipeg, Canada.

Mayer M (1955). *They Thought They Were Free: The Germans 1933-45.* The University of Chicago Press, Chicago.

Maynard ML (1855). *The Studies and Teaching of the Society of Jesus at the Time of Its Suppression, 1750-1773.* John Murphy and Company, Baltimore.

McGauley J (2015). 13 Everyday Items You Never Knew Were Made by Prisoners. https://www.thrillist.com/gear/products-made-by-prisoners-clothing-furniture-electronics. Accessed and vetted 06 November 2016.

Melby T (2016). MPRNews: Sex Abuse Victims Say Minn. Law Brought Hope, Chance for Justice. http://www.mprnews.org/story/2016/05/25/sex-abuse-victims-say-minnesota-law-brought-hope. Accessed and vetted 06 November 2016.

Mendham J Reverend (1834). *Memoirs of the Council of Trent; Principally Derived From Manuscript and Unpublished Records, Namely, Histories, Diaries, letters, and Other Documents of the Leading Actors in That Assembly.* James Duncan, London.

Michelet J (1845). Priests, Women and Families. Longman, Brown, Green and Longmans, London.

Michelet J and Quinet E, with Lester CE, Translator (1845). *The Jesuits.* Gates and Stedman, New York.

Mierins AM (2002). University of New Hampshire Law Review: Review of "Law in America: A Short History," by Lawrence M. Friedman. http://scholars.unh.edu/cgi/viewcontent.cgi?article=1024&context=unh_lr. Accessed and vetted 06 November 2016.

Mitchell PA (n.d.). "31 Questions and Answers About the Internal Revenue Service", rev. 3.7, Seattle, WA. www.supremelaw.org/sls/31answers.htm. Accessed and vetted 07 November 2016.

Mohney G (2015). ABC News: Heroin-Related Deaths Quadruple As Drug Epidemic Continues to Impact U.S. http://abcnews.go.com/Health/heroin-related-deaths-quadruple-drug-epidemic-continues-impact/story?id=32285495. Accessed and vetted 06 November 2016.

Monk M and Slocum JJ Reverend, Revised by (1851). *Awful Disclosures by Maria Monk of the Hotel Dieu Nunnery of Montreal; with An Appendix; and a Supplement Giving More Particulars of the Nunnery and Grounds, 3rd Edition.* James S. Hodson, London.

Monk M. (1855). *Awful Disclosures by Maria Monk of the Hotel Dieu Nunnery of Montreal. Containing Also, Many Incidents Never Before Published.* De Witt and Davenport Publishers, New York.

Montagu R Lord (1877). *Foreign Policy: England and the Eastern Question.* Chapman and Hall, London.

Moore E (1941). *No Friend of Democracy.* International Publishing Company, London.

Morris R (1883). *Robert Morgan; or, Political Anti-Masonry, It's Rise, Growth and Decadence.* Robert Macoy, Masonic Publisher, New York.

Morse SFB (1835). *Foreign Conspiracy Against the Liberties of the United States.* Leavitt, Lord and Company, New York.

Morse SFB 1855. *Foreign Conspiracy Against the Liberties of the United States.* American and Foreign Christian Union, New York.

Moylan M (2016). Next Mission for Twin Cities Archdiocese: Life after Bankruptcy. http://www.mprnews.org/story/2016/05/19/twin-cities-archdiocese-readies-post-bankruptcy-plan. Accessed and vetted 06 November 2016.

Mullins E (1991). *Secrets of the Federal Reserve: The London Connection.* Bridger House Publishers, Inc., Carson City.

Mumford SD (1984). *American Democracy & The Vatican: Population Growth & National Security.* Humanist Press, Amherst, NY.

Murray OE PhD Reverend (1892). *The Black Pope or the Jesuits' Conspiracy Against American Institutions*, 2nd Edition. The Patriot Company, Chicago.

Neuman S (2015). NPR: Archdiocese Of St. Paul-Minneapolis Files Chapter 11. http://www.npr.org/sections/thetwo-way/2015/01/16/377732977/archdiocese-of-st-paul-minneapolis-files-chapter-11. Accessed and vetted 06 November 2016.

Newdegate CN (1880). *A Glimpse of the Great Secret Society.* Hatchards, Piccadilly, London.

Nicolini GB (1854). *History of the Jesuits: Their Origin, Progress, Doctrines, and Designs.* Henry Bohn, London.

Osburn W (1846). *Hidden Works of Darkness, or, The Doings of the Jesuits.* WH Dalton, published for the Protestant Association, London.

O'Sullivan M Reverend and M'Ghee R Reverend (1840). *Romanism As It Rules In Ireland.* RB Seeley and William Burnside, London.

Our Time.org (2016). Why private prisons are more likely to house more people of color. http://www.ourtime.org/news/why-private-prisons-are-even-more-likely-than-public-prisons-to-house-people-of-color-2/. Accessed and vetted 06 November 2016.

Overbury RW (1846). *The Jesuits.* Houlston and Stoneman, London.

Owen RL (1919). *Where Is God in the European War?* The Century Company, New York.

Paris E (1975). *The Secret History of the Jesuits.* Chick Publications, Chino, CA.

Parkman F (1867). *France and England in North America: A Series of Historical Narratives, Part Second*. Little, Brown, and Company, Boston.

Parkman F (1902). *The Jesuits in North America in the Seventeenth Century, Part One*. Little, Brown, and Company, Boston.

Pascal B (1892). *Provincial Letters: Moral Teachings of the Jesuit Fathers Opposed to the Church of Rome and Latin Vulgate*. William Briggs, Montreal.

Perverter (1851). *The Perverter in High Life: A True Narrative of Jesuit Duplicity*. Partridge and Oakey, London.

Pitrat JC (1855). *Americans Warned of Jesuitism, or The Jesuits Unveiled, 3rd Edition*. Edward W. Hinks and Company, Boston.

Plaisted DA (2006). Estimates of the Number Killed by the Papacy in the Middle Ages and later. http://www.cs.unc.edu/~plaisted/ estimates.html. Accessed and vetted 06 November 2016.

Pollard AF (1892). *The Jesuits in Poland*. Methuen and Company. London.

Pollen JH SJ (1896). *The Life and Letters of Father John Morris of the Society of Jesus*. Burnes and Oates, Ltd., London.

Pollen JH SJ (1896). *The Counter-Reformation in Scotland, with Special Reference to the Revival of 1585 to 1595*. Sands and Company, London.

Pollen JH SJ (1901). *Papal Negotiations with Mary Queen of Scots During Her Reign in Scotland, 1561-1567*. University Press Edinburgh for the Scottish History Society, Edinburgh.

Pollen JH SJ (1920). *The English Catholics in the Reign of Queen Elizabeth: A Study of Their Politics, Civil Life and Government.* Longmans, Green and Company, London.

Pollen JH SJ (1922). *Saint Ignatius of Loyola: Imitator of Christ, 1494 to 1555.* PJ Kennedy and Sons, New York.

Pollen JH SJ (1922). *Mary Queen of Scots and The Babington Plot.* University Press Edinburgh for the Scottish History Society, Edinburgh.

Pommells M (2014). Study: More People of Color Sentenced to Private Prisons Than Whites. http://www.huffingtonpost.com/michaela-pommells/study-more-people-of-colo_b_4826086.html/. Accessed and vetted 06 November 2016.

Protestant Association (1834). *The Jesuits Exposed, 2nd Edition, Volume 15.* The Protestant Association, London.

Quandt KR (2014). Why There's an Even Larger Racial Disparity in Private Prisons Than in Public Ones. http://www.motherjones.com/mojo/2014/01/even-larger-racial-disparity-private-prisons-public-prisons. Accessed and vetted 06 November 2016.

Quigley C (1966). *Tragedy and Hope: A History of the World in Our Time.* The Macmillan Company, New York.

Reed H Reverend (1874). *The Footprints of Satan: or, The Devil in History.* EB Treat, New York.

Renich KL (1914). *The Life and Methods of Matteo Ricci, Jesuits Missionary to China, 1582-1610.* Master of Arts in History Thesis, The Graduate School, University of Illinois.

Ridgeway J (2012). Smackdown: ACLU Calls Out Private Prison Giant. http://www.motherjones.com/mojo/2012/05/aclu-challenges-private-prison-company-cca. Accessed and vetted 06 November 2016.

Robison J (1798). *Proofs of a Conspiracy Against All the Religions and Governments of Europe, Carried on in the Secret Meetings of Free Masons, Iluminati, and Reading Societies. Collected from Good Authorities.* T Dobson, Philadelphia.

Roper IH (1848). *The Jesuits*, 2nd Edition. Houlston and Stoneman, London.

Rule WH Reverend (1853). *Celebrated Jesuits*, Volume I. John Mason, London.

Rule WH Reverend (1853). *Celebrated Jesuits, Volume II.* John Mason, London.

Salzillo L (2016). Daily Kos: Trucker Saves Victim of Torture at a PILOT Station After Recognizing the Signs of Sex Trafficking. http://www.dailykos.com/stories/2016/6/24/1542136/-Trucker-saves-victim-of-torture-at-a-PILOT-station-after-recognizing-the-signs-of-sex-trafficking. https://polarisproject.org. Accessed and vetted 06 November 2016.

Saussy TF (1999). *Rulers of Evil: Useful Knowledge About Governing Bodies.* Ospray Bookmakers, Nevada.

Scahill, J (2007). Project Censored: #7 Behind Blackwater Inc. http://projectcensored.org/7-behind-blackwater-inc/. Accessed and vetted 06 November 2016.

Schweizer P (2012). Contributions of Christopher Clavius SJ to Mathematics. *Gerbertus*, 2.

Schwickerath R SJ (1903). *Jesuit Education: Its History and Principles.* B. Herder, St. Louis.

Seager C (1847). *The Spiritual Exercises of St. Ignatius of Loyola* (Translator). Charles Dolman, London.

Sherman EA 32° Scottish Mason (1883). *The Engineer Corps of Hell, or, Rome's Sappers and Miners.* Edwin Allen Sherman, San Francisco.

Skousen WC (1970). *The Naked Capitalist: A Review and Commentary on Dr. Carroll Quigley's Book: Tragedy and Hope–A History of the World in Our Time.* Privately published by W. Cleon Skousen, Salt Lake City.

Sloan B (2015). Identifying Businesses That Profit From Prison Labor. https://www.popularresistance.org/identifying-businesses-that-profit-from-prison-labor/. Accessed and vetted 06 November 2016.

Smith CM and Rasor D (2012). Self-Dealing and the War Service Industry, Part I. http://www.truth-out.org/news/item/8324-self-dealing-and-the-war-service-industry-part-i?tmpl=component&print=1. Accessed and vetted 06 November 2016.

Spencer J Editor (1670). *The Jesuits Morals: by a Doctor of the Colledge of School of Paris who hath faithfully extracted them out of the Jesuits own books, which are printed by the permission and approbation of the superiours of their society.* John Starkey, London.

Stein J (2008). Dick Cheney Is Not Going to Prison. http://www.motherjones.com/mojo/2008/11/dick-cheney-not-going-prison. Accessed and vetted 06 November 2016.

Steinmetz A (1846). *The Novitiate, or, A Year Among the English Jesuits*. Smith, Elder and Company, London.

Steinmetz A (1848). *History of the Jesuits: From the Foundation of Their Society to its Suppression by Pope Clement XIV.; Their Missions Throughout the World; Their Educational System and Literature; With Their Revival and Present State, Part I*. Richard Bentley, London.

Steinmetz A (1848). *History of the Jesuits: From the Foundation of Their Society to its Suppression by Pope Clement XIV.; Their Missions Throughout the World; Their Educational System and Literature; With Their Revival and Present State, Part II*. Richard Bentley, London.

Steinmetz A (1848). *History of the Jesuits: From the Foundation of Their Society to its Suppression by Pope Clement XIV.; Their Missions Throughout the World; Their Educational System and Literature; With Their Revival and Present State, Part III*. Richard Bentley, London.

Stumo M (2016). http://www.flushthetpp.org/peterson-institute-report-on-the-tpp-is-faulty/. The Coalition for a Prosperous America. Accessed and vetted 06 November 2016.

Swenson C (2008). *Organized Chaos: An Illustrated Record of Greed, Corruption, Confusion and Conspiracy*. J&M Printing, Inc.

Taunton EL (1901). *The History of the Jesuits in England, 1580–1773*. Lippincott, Philadelphia.

Tayler WE (1851). *Popery: Its Character and Its Crimes*. Partridge and Oakley, London.

Thompson F (1913). *Saint Ignatius Loyola*. Burns and Oats, London.

Thompson RW (1894). *Footprints of the Jesuits*. Cranston and Curts, New York.

Thwaites RG Editor (1897). *The Jesuit Relations and Allied Documents: Travels and Explorations of the Jesuit Missionaries in New France, 1610-1791*. The Burrows Brothers Company, Cleveland.

Trevor W (1972). *In the Public Interest*. Scriptures Unlimited, Los Angeles.

Tyson AS (2014). U.S. Firm Taps Ex Operators to Fight ISIS. http://www.scout.com/military/warrior/story/1487723-u-s-firm-taps-ex-operators-to-fight-isis. Accessed and vetted 06 November 2016.

Udias A and Stauder W (2002). The Jesuit Contribution to Seismology. *International Handbook of Earthquake and Engineering Seismology*, Volume 81A, pp. 19-27.

United Nations Treaty Series (2002) *Rome Statute of the International Criminal Court*. International Criminal Court, The Hague.

Villers C (1833). *An Essay on the Spirit and Influence of the Reformation* (Miller S, Translator). Key and Biddle, Philadelphia.

Wade L PhD (2013). 100 Iconic American Companies Exploiting Prisoners to Sell You Products. https://mic.com/articles/33691/100-iconic-american-companies-exploiting-prisoners-to-sell-you-products#.PrGywm7OF. Accessed and vetted 06 November 2016.

Wadswort J (1679). *The Memoirs of James Wadswort, a Jesuit That Recanted: Discovering a Dreadful Prophesy of Impiety, and Blasphemous Doctrines (or Gospel) of the Jesuits, With Their Antithetical Lives and Conversations.* Henry Brome, London.

Walsh W (1903). *The Jesuits in Great Britain: An Historical Inquiry into their Political Influence.* George Routledge. London.

Watson TE (1912). *The Life and Times of Andrew Jackson.* The Jeffersonian Publishing Company, Thomson, GA.

Watson TE (1928). *Roman Catholics in America Falsifying History and Poisoning the Minds of Protestant School Children.* Tom Watson Book Company, Thomson, GA.

Watson TE (1928). *Rome's Law Or Ours? Which?* Tom Watson Book Company, Thomson, GA.

Watson TE (1928). *The 4th Degree Oath of the Knights of Columbus: An Un-American Secret Society Bound to the Italian Pope, By Pledges of Treason and Murder.* Tom Watson Book Company, Thomson, GA.

Watson TE (1927). *Maria Monk and Her Revelations of Convent Crimes, 2nd Edition.* Tom Watson Book Company, Thomson, GA.

Week Staff (2012). The Week: How pixelated uniforms turned soldiers into walking targets. http://theweek.com/articles/474260/how-pixelated-uniforms-turned-soldiers-into-walking-targets. Accessed and vetted 06 November 2016.

Wells S (2013). *Drunk with Blood: God's Killings in the Bible.* SAB Books, Moscow, ID.

White JG Reverend (1890). *Footprints of Satan: Pope and Jesuits Against Bible and Public Schools.* JG White, Boston.

Whitehead M (2013). *English Jesuit Education: Expulsion, Suppression, Survival and Restoration, 1762-1803.* Ashgate Publishing, Ltd., Surrey.

Wylie JA Reverend (1852). *The Papacy: Its History, Dogma, Genius and Prospects.* Hamilton, Adams and Company, London.

Wylie JA Reverend (1855). *Pilgrimage from Alps to the Tiber.* Hamilton, Adams and Company, London.

Wylie JA (1902). *The History of Protestantism,* Volumes I, II and III. Cassell, Petter and Galpin, London.

Wylie JA Reverend (1886). *History of the Scottish Nation,* Volume I. Hamilton, Adams and Company, London.

Wylie JA Reverend (1887). *History of the Scottish Nation,* Volume II. Hamilton, Adams and Company, London.

Wylie JA Reverend (1890). *History of the Scottish Nation,* Volume III. Hamilton, Adams and Company, London.

Wylie JA Reverend (1860). *Ter-Centenary of the Scottish Reformation.* John Maclaren, Edinburgh.

Wylie JA Reverend (1878). *The Papal Hierarchy: An Exposure of the Tactics of Rome for the Overthrow of the Liberty and Christianity of Great Britain.* Hamilton, Adams and Company, London.

Wylie JA Reverend (1866). *The Awakening of Italy, and the Crisis of Rome.* The Religious Tract Society, London.

Wylie JA (1870). *Daybreak in Spain: Sketches of Spain and Its New Reformation*. Cassell, Petter and Galpin, London.

Wylie JA Reverend (1867). *The Papacy*. Hamilton, Adams and Company, London.

Wylie JA Reverend (1865). *Rome on Civil Liberty*. Hamilton, Adams and Company, London.

Wylie JA (1881). *The Jesuits: Their Moral Maxims, and Plots Against Kings, Nations, and Churches. With Dissertation on Ireland*. Hamilton, Adams, and Company, London.

Wylie JA Reverend (1899). *The History of Protestantism*. Cassell and Company, Limited, London.